THE CAPTAIN CALLED IT MUTINY

THE U. S. BRIG-OF-WAR SOMERS.

The caption reads: "A mutiny was discovered on board this vessel Nov. 26th 1842, while on her homeward voyage from the coast of Africa, and the three ringleaders, Philip Spencer, midshipman, Samuel A. Cromwell, boatswain's mate, and Elijah H. Small, seaman, were hung at the yard arm, Dec. 1st 1842, which completely suppressed the mutiny." *Courtesy of Kennedy Galleries.*

FREDERIC F. VAN DE WATER

The Captain Called It
MUTINY

IVES WASHBURN, INC., NEW YORK

To Edward Terhune Van de Water
with affection and admiration

Acknowledgment

Citation is feeble thanks to offer the many persons whose generosity expedited the creation of this book. Among its author's principal creditors are:

Mr. Franklin Brandreth, Albany, New York;

Captain Wade De Weese, U.S.N. (ret.), director, U.S. Naval Academy Museum;

Rear Admiral Daniel V. Gallery, U.S.N.;

Mr. Robert W. Hill, Keeper of Manuscripts, New York Public Library;

Mrs. Robert Longueil, Brattleboro, Vermont;

Mrs. Alice M. Runyon, Associate Director, Sleepy Hollow Restorations, Tarrytown, New York;

Mr. E. Seger Slifer, National Secretary, Chi Psi Fraternity;

Mrs. Benjamin O. Warren, Librarian, Warner Library, Tarrytown, New York.

Finally, and climactically, a particular debt hereby is acknowledged to Mr. Sylvester L. Vigilante, Chief of the American History Division, New York Public Library; Professor Louis H. Bolander, Librarian, U.S. Naval Academy, and Mrs. Nelson E. Withington, Brattleboro, Vermont, for wisdom, patience, and inestimable aid.

FREDERIC F. VAN DE WATER

West Dummerston, Vermont

Foreword

During the 112 years that have passed since the officers of
the U.S. Brig *Somers* sentenced three of their shipmates to be
hanged for mutiny, that singular episode has been largely
ignored, possibly because it is human instinct to overlook
matters that resist neat explanations. Though a long succes-
sion of witnesses described the event, their suspiciously
harmonious testimony failed to hide entirely certain funda-
mentals that deny the existence of a mutiny. These obdurate
facts still remain unaltered, and it has been this narrative's
intention to present them carefully and completely.

The book has been a long time a-borning. Its gestation may
have begun more than a century ago when its author's great-
uncle, while imprisoned as a suspected mutineer, wrote his
own prejudiced account of his experiences. His papers have
come down through three generations to their present owner.
More lately, a collection of books and papers, assembled by
the author's father-in-law, the late William W. Gay, newspaperman, bibliophile, and loyal member of Chi Psi Fraternity,
had added substance and stature to what otherwise might
have remained a dim family legend.

As the volume has taken shape, its author has felt increasingly the imperative need to stress its factual nature. Though
cast in narrative form, the tale is not fiction. The bizarre happenings that constitute the *Somers* affair are more thoroughly
documented than many better-known episodes in American
history.

Verbatim transcripts of the court of inquiry and of the subsequent court-martial that considered the case still exist. Most of the material hereafter presented has been based on these.

Excerpts from such primary sources have been printed in italics. Conversation occasionally has been transposed from indirect quotation to direct for the sake of emphasis, but in no instance has its purport been altered.

If the following account of the *Somers* "mutiny" seems preposterously fantastic, its narrator only can maintain that it could not sound otherwise, since the conduct of many involved in the event attained a degree of irrationality beyond the possibility of further exaggeration.

FREDERIC F. VAN DE WATER

West Dummerston, Vermont

Contents

THE CAPTAIN CALLED IT MUTINY

CHAPTER 1

Revelation

"Captain Mackenzie and his officers acted at the time under a species of insanity, produced by panic, lively imagination and the spirit of the age, all working together."—JAMES GORDON BENNETT.

THE BRIG was a dark particle, enclosed by the twin immensities of sky and ocean, a small and lonely entity that crept through the brilliant azure of the Spanish Main beneath a lid of paler blue where serried clouds of the trade wind marched.

She was low and lean, and her sides were studded with guns. Inward-sweeping counter and keen bows extending into a lancelike bowsprit and jib boom gave her a piratical aspect, befitting her presence on seas where a scummy residue of the ancient buccaneering brotherhood still furtively pillaged. The brig showed no flag; another suspicious circumstance. Her pace, too, was puzzling.

Plainly, she had been built for speed, yet she idled along in a fair breeze with mainsail furled and less than half her normal canvas drawing. How could she be loitering, or lurking, for any honest purpose?

It was a little after midday of Thursday, December 1, 1842. No looming storm, no threat of reef or shoal justified the craft's hesitant progress across the threshold of the Caribbean. The nearest of the islands were two days' sailing to the westward. A faint bruise on the eastern horizon might indicate the approach of a thunder shower but it was still far away.

The wind blew sweetly; the brig slouched over the white-edged rollers. A long-gathering tempest was about to break aboard the craft, and her company of men and boys had been massed at her waist to witness and implement the outburst.

Smoke, blue white, jetted from the brig's flank, and the thump of a carronade ran over the sunny water. There was sudden movement along her deck and grotesque invasion of the air above it.

Three hooded and manacled beings went up through emptiness toward the main yardarm. They swung, black oblongs against the noontide brilliance, and when the lines that had noosed their necks had been drawn to their utmost, they dangled inertly below the furled sail. After an interval, the sound of shrill cheering came from the brig.

A flag had crept to the gaff of the craft's stern sail and had blossomed in the wind. It was not the grisly white-and-black emblem of buccaneers. It was vividly striped and starred.

The men and boys who were sent below to dinner while the three dead still rocked at the yardarm were neither pirates nor lawless seafarers of any breed. They were the duly enlisted crew of the United States Brig-of-War *Somers*, lately transformed into a school ship. Her captain, Alexander Slidell Mackenzie, Commander, U.S.N., with endorsement by his officers, had ordered the hangings of three ringleaders in a mutiny.

Two of the executed were humble men: Boatswain's Mate Samuel Cromwell and Seaman Elisha Small. The third, and the alleged instigator of a plot to take the brig and turn her into a sea raider, was Acting Midshipman Philip Spencer, an eighteen-year-old scapegrace. Beyond his unconfirmed rank and his sponsorship of the conspiracy—if there were a conspiracy—he had no personal distinction, yet in hanging him Mackenzie reached far and dared greatly.

Young Philip was the son of the secretary of war in the cabinet of John Tyler, then president of the United States, and John Canfield Spencer was a notoriously vindictive and politically influential man.

The drama that reached its terrific climax on the afterdeck of the *Somers,* that bright tropical midday 112 years ago, might have remained memorable solely for the mystery and the epidemic terror that distort its outlines. There are better reasons why it should not be forgotten:

The *Somers* affair is the only mutiny recorded in the United States Navy since the Constitution was ratified.

It was the pristine force that brought about the establishment of the Naval Academy at Annapolis.

It drove at least one man to suicide; created a protracted enmity between two members of Tyler's cabinet; painfully disturbed the navy's high brass; roused James Fenimore Cooper to one of his more violent eruptions; distressed Washington Irving, patron of the brig's commander, and became, for unnumbered others, a terminus to friendships and a starting point for feuds.

Finally, a highly distorted version of the tragic episode was incorporated into the ritual of the Chi Psi fraternity, which Philip Spencer had helped to found.

Slighter and less important episodes in the national annals have not been so generally disregarded; nor, when they have been dredged out of the past, have they been equally beclouded by misstatement and prejudice.

When the crew had dined and the bodies of the dead had

been committed piously to the sea, the brig's captain still found himself oppressed by problems and tensions. He was convinced that the executions he had ordered had beheaded a mutinous conspiracy, but he still had four alleged plotters under arrest whose guilt did not seem sufficiently proven to warrant more hangings.

These four captives were kept, heavily ironed and closely guarded, on the quarter-deck, since their commander could think of no better place to stow them. They were obstacles to the smooth working of the vessel, and Mackenzie considered them a latent menace. He, and indeed the brig's entire company, was still rocked by the ground swell of recent terror.

The *Somers* had been bound from Monrovia, Liberia, to St. Thomas in the Virgin Islands, for provisioning. Her captain supplied her as quickly as possible in that port and then set the craft winging north to her home station, New York.

Mackenzie felt certain there were still incipient mutineers not yet executed or arrested on board the brig. He had had the possessions of the three hanged men searched, and no further evidence implicating others had been discovered, yet the morbid belief persisted.

The captain of the *Somers* did all in his power to avert an uprising. Lest his prisoners, by night, should manage to communicate with the disaffected still at large, Mackenzie ordered that man-size bags of sailcloth be made, with drawstrings at their throats. Each evening when darkness approached, the four wretched captives were thrust into these oversized purses, which were then tied above their heads to ensure their safe-keeping till morning.

If the men thus enclosed were half smothered, that was— unfortunate. Later, when storms of the northern latitudes filled the bags with sea water and threatened to drown their contents, the prisoners were removed from the quarter-deck and penned up below.

The commander exercised himself still further to pacify his crew. He preached to them during Sunday muster, denouncing sin, praising virtue, and exhorting them to stand firm. During the last reach of the long voyage, he added further suspects to his collection until he had eleven men in irons.

There is no evidence that, before these arrests, any further disaffection had arisen to justify them; no way of determining, now, why the additional seven men were made captive. It may have been that the commander felt it would be easier to persuade authority that the executions of Spencer, Cromwell, and Small had been imperative if he still had a number of unhanged prisoners on hand. Family pride inclines me to favor this possibility, for one of the alleged culprits, so tardily adorned with leg irons and manacles, was my own great-uncle.

In 1838, George Walgrove Warner of New York, at the age of seventeen, had run off and joined the navy to get away from a stern stepmother. Nothing of a definitely incriminating nature was ever pinned on my ancestor, but he appreciated his imprisonment so little that, on his release, he eagerly reunited himself with his family, stepmother or no stepmother, and never again went to sea.

Not a formidable mutineer, my unsainted great-uncle, but he soothed himself while in jail by writing a good deal about the *Somers* mutiny and what he clearly considered his own undeserved treatment. Some of these reflections still survive and faintly illuminate a few of the case's many obscurities.

Warner was not the sole member of the brig's company to relieve intense internal pressure with a pen. While the *Somers* climbed the latitudes from summery Caribbean weather into the gales and sleet of the North Atlantic, Alexander Slidell Mackenzie frequently found time to spend at his desk.

The commander was preparing his report on the recent tragedy for Abel P. Upshur, secretary of the navy, and believed himself particularly fitted for the task. For years, when not too peremptorily distracted by his profession, Mackenzie had made writing his avocation and was already the author of six books. Though the literary worth of these was moderate, the commander might have spared himself much anguish and other persons still greater torment if he had resigned from the navy and bent the entire energy of his peculiar mind to the production of beautiful letters.

It is unlikely that any such thought disturbed the mind of Alexander Slidell Mackenzie while he sat in his heaving cabin and happily plied his pen. The man was never discernibly unsatisfied with himself. Beyond doubt, he was pleased by the resounding, if frequently redundant, periods he was creating.

"*Nothing is more apparent,*" the chronically irascible James Fenimore Cooper wrote, "*than the fact that Commander Mackenzie in his report intended to favor the world with a fine and memorable description; one that would be quoted in after ages for its thrilling incidents and graphic beauty.*"

The commander was generous with his artistry. Though the creation of pure fiction was beyond his ability, he was always inclined to cover the severely functional duties of naval command with antimacassars of romance and sentiment. His report of the triple hanging he had decreed is frequently imaginative and adorned with sentimental furbelows. It is hard to decide in this singular narrative where the commander yields to the author or vice versa. Each continually trespassed upon the other's province in all Mackenzie's activities.

His perpetual blending of profession and avocation invested

the safe return of the *Somers* to her home port with trappings so romantic that her arrival more nearly resembled the beginning of a three-volume novel than a naval maneuver.

A long, low craft with sloping masts stole in through the Narrows toward dusk of Tuesday, December 14, 1842, and found a remote anchorage in the lower harbor. A boat was stealthily lowered. A figure muffled in a cape embarked and was swiftly rowed to the New Jersey shore. Thereafter, the brig kept her station until her captain was certain that his lieutenant, Guert Gansevoort, grandson of Peter, the Revolutionary general, had accomplished his mission.

No one else left the brig; no one was permitted to board her. She remained aloof and mysterious, while ample time elapsed for her lieutenant to reach Washington, via the railroad from South Amboy, and to deliver Commander Mackenzie's calamitous dispatch to Secretary Upshur.

So complete was the secrecy the *Somers'* captain imposed that his vessel's arrival in the bay and her subsequent cryptic behavior were almost entirely ignored by the New York newspapers. They were to make ample amends later for that neglect.

The *Somers* made sail, Thursday, December 16, and walked up to the Brooklyn Navy Yard with her dire tale still untold. Great-uncle George and his fellow miscreants were jailed aboard the receiving ship, *North Carolina*. The unimprisoned members of the brig's crew, as well as those in irons, were denied any contact with the civilian world that was turning merrily toward the holiday season.

Mackenzie hoped to keep the story of the mutiny and its aftermath hermetically sealed until he had received a reply to his report from the Secretary of the Navy, but despite precautions, someone talked.

The day after the *Somers'* arrival at the navy yard, the

Morning Courier and Enquirer carried a brief and excessively garbled story of the tragedy. The newspaper's proprietor, the bewhiskered and elegant Colonel J. Watson Webb, was Mackenzie's friend and neighbor. He occupied a home adjoining the commander's farm in what is now North Tarrytown, New York.

The colonel's beat, though grossly inaccurate, set other papers baying on the trail and popular excitement soaring. No further information could be obtained immediately. The *Somers*, at her navy yard berth, could not be boarded by reporters, and her captain, who was at the home of his brother-in-law, Commodore Matthew Calbraith Perry, commandant of the navy yard, would see no one.

Mackenzie was too busy to be interrupted. He was hard at work upon another, more complete and elegant narrative of the tragedy. He had a soon-to-be justified belief that the Secretary of the Navy would demand a still fuller report on the executions than the dispatch Gansevoort had borne to Washington.

Sunday and the news blank it imposed gave an aroused citizenry ample opportunity to blow up still further an already distorted tale. Philip Spencer was pictured as a black villain and Alexander Slidell Mackenzie as a righteous Ajax who had defied the thunderbolts of the Secretary of War through a stern sense of rectitude and a Roman devotion to duty.

The commander, this day, boosted his reputation still higher in the popular mind by marching the unhanged and unarrested remainder of his crew to the navy yard chapel, there to give thanks for their deliverance from monstrous peril. Mackenzie, in dress uniform, led the little blue column to and from services.

By Monday morning, December 20, all the papers had the

stupefying news in more correct detail, and they employed it profligately. The tale of mutiny and intended piracy pushed other tidings off front pages and was discussed explosively in editorial columns. Never had the still-provincial press of a metropolis-to-be dealt with so sensational a story, and editors played it to their utmost. There was warrant for their frenzy.

The *Somers* tragedy fitted its era and the taste of 1842 readers. It was a period piece, faithful to the standards set by Gothic tales of its time. All the customary ingredients were present: a mad plot that moved a set of unlikely characters along from one wild act to a still more extravagant; an unearthly terror, feeding upon itself; and, spread over the demented proceedings and increasing their horror, a brittle glaze of piety and patriotism.

Nothing else so irrational can be found in American archives; nothing so fantastic yet grimly factual; nothing so preposterous yet solidly documented as this nightmare that boarded a United States brig-of-war and, for five days of mounting terror, drove men to excesses of cowardice and brutality.

The events of the mutiny, when set in sequence, do achieve a kind of coherence; yet most of them, even when so ordered, elude a sober appraisal. Logic that a factual presentation requires, motivation that a fictional version would demand, are equally unattainable. Hazard and surmise, stretched to their utmost, cannot clothe the tale in coherence. It escapes from prosaic history into the realm of the wildly implausible and, but for the fact that the dreadfulness actually did happen, would be dismissed as a manifest impossibility.

The *Somers* case is a study of fear that, parentless as Melchizedek and contagious as the plague, corrupted the spirits of theretofore reputable men and, while the obsession endured, made poltroons of them. Though the narrative lacks the symmetry of classic tragedy or the outright chaos of insanity, elements of each are apparent in the story of the mysterious seizure that debased officers of the United States Navy and turned the vessel they commanded into a sea-borne madhouse.

What sort of men were the principal antagonists whose conflict wrought this bedlam? One was a pious, tedious, rather prudish man whose record, until then, had been blameless. The other was a surly boy of eighteen who, before this fell association, had achieved little that was praiseworthy and had committed only venial sins.

Why, in conjunction, did Alexander Slidell Mackenzie and Philip Spencer create this infectious and monstrous frenzy? The tragedy they acted out together lay not in their stars but in themselves. All that is known of either man today cannot reveal entirely the mutually destructive elements in their natures.

CHAPTER 2

Principal Characters

*"Captain Mackenzie enjoyed probably a much higher liter-
ary reputation than he merited. . . . His place in the corps was
not sufficiently high to create envy, or sufficiently low to produce indifference."*—JAMES FENIMORE COOPER.

A ROMANTIC tradition requires that there be a hero and a
villain in every conflict. A further convention holds that if the
character of one adversary be far from admirable, by necessity,
the nature of the other is praiseworthy.

The tumult the *Somers* case aroused in its time came largely
from adherents to this seesaw dogma. Good and evil were not
plainly opposed in the strife between the brig's captain and his
recalcitrant acting midshipman, yet opinions that lowered
Mackenzie's reputation responsively exalted Philip Spencer's.

The commander, though he illegally destroyed the boy and
his two alleged accomplices, thereby did not reveal himself as
a complete scoundrel, nor did the young man quite qualify for
the rank of martyr defenders have conferred on him. Slayer
and slain alike were composed of more than usually faulty, if
divergent, materials. Each in his own way was so fallible that
it is impossible completely to justify either.

By his own written words, Mackenzie reveals himself as one
of the more unpleasant minor personages in our national history, but Spencer, judged by the witless enterprises of his short
life, was a sulky incorrigible. Spencer's unendearing character

is easier to explain than the ornate complexities of the com-mander's. Sympathy goes more readily to the comprehensible than to the cryptic being and to a youthful victim than to a mature victor.

Apologists for Spencer a century ago and his junior brethren in Chi Psi fraternity who canonized him without benefit of clergy conformed to a national ethic. He was the underdog that it has always been American instinct to defend. Mac-kenzie was an embodiment of arbitrary authority, which is still generally suspect in the republic. Additionally, the commander possessed personal qualities that did not lift him in popular esteem.

Alexander Slidell Mackenzie was in 1842, when Horace Greeley saw him, *"a man of medium height, with a fine head covered rather thinly with light auburn hair, a high forehead and of an amiable and pleasing, rather than stern and com-manding, presence."*

The commander then was thirty-nine years old. His appear-ance, even in the full uniform he wore on all possible occa-sions, was disconcertingly mild, considering the scandal he provoked. He bore no physical resemblance, despite the loud insistences of partisans, to a hero or a tyrant.

Probably, Mackenzie was neither one nor the other. He was a prudish, overimaginative person, equipped with more than the usual Victorian collection of poses, a man of exquisitely tender vanity whose ambitions outran his abilities. When he was caught in a chain of events that he was too small to handle, it was inevitable that he should make a shocking mess of them, and his later frantic attempts to justify himself further lessened his never considerable stature.

The captain of the *Somers* had been born Alexander Slidell.

His parents were John Slidell, a New York merchant in more than comfortable circumstances, and Margaret Mackenzie Slidell, a Scotswoman with a wealthy bachelor brother, Alexander Mackenzie. In later years he offered to pay the then Lieutenant Slidell, U.S.N., well if he would assume his mother's maiden name. In 1839, the officer obligingly, by act of legislature, became Alexander Slidell Mackenzie, thereby exchanging his birth name for a less distinguished if more rewarding.

The Slidells in their own persons and by advantageous marriages were an influential family. Alexander's father was the first president of both the Mechanics Bank of New York and the Traders Fire Insurance Company. His son John, Junior, migrated to Louisiana, where he was chosen successively a representative in Congress, minister to Mexico, United States senator, and during the Civil War, in association with James M. Mason, Confederate commissioner to France. Another son, Thomas, became chief justice of the Louisiana Supreme Court.

Alexander's sister, Jane Slidell, was the wife of Matthew Galbraith Perry, soon to be instrumental in opening up Japan to western trade and a power in the navy. A Slidell aunt married William A. Duer, president of Columbia College.

It may have been Perry's example that inspired Alexander Slidell, at the age of twelve, to apply for a midshipman's warrant. He was to have no further schooling than the service's narrow professional education. Years later, he wrote that he had been *"trained almost from infancy in a profession which rendered connected study impossible"* and had got *"what little education has fallen to me in much the same discursive and vagabond manner that a chicken gets his breakfast—a kernel of information in one corner and another in the next."*

The confession is one of Mackenzie's rare recorded approaches to jest. He found humor in few matters and never in himself.

His naval service was distinguished principally by sober industry, which won him no particular renown, and by his ability, thanks to his family's affluence, to spend long leaves in European travel. The commander-to-be was midshipman aboard the light frigate *Macedonian* of the Pacific Squadron from 1818 to 1822. When, in 1824, Commodore David Porter sailed south with a task force to clean out the pirates still infesting West Indian waters, Mackenzie went with him aboard the three-gun *Terrier*, a converted Chesapeake Bay schooner.

It was a fateful assignment for the impressionable youngster. The seagoing gangsters who still sneaked about the Spanish Main were degenerate descendants of the great buccaneers—a mongrel, largely Latin pack who massacred the weak and fled from the strong.

For Alexander Slidell Mackenzie pirates thenceforth were to be not merely figures in lurid romances but actual and dreadful beings of appalling savagery. His vivid recollection of them and their depredations was among the forces that were to impel him to hang three members of his own command on a still far-off December afternoon.

Ten years after he had joined the navy, Midshipman Slidell got his lieutenancy. He celebrated his promotion by taking a long leave in Spain.

Something beside his zeal distinguished young Slidell from his fellow officers. Early in his career, he had been beset by the itch to write. Later, he won more notice through the practice of his avocation than, lacking his unfortunate association with Philip Spencer, his professional accomplishments were likely to have gained him.

If books by the sailor-author were imitative and short-lived, that did not lessen his repute in the eyes of his brethren in the service. It made small difference to them whether Lieutenant Slidell wrote originally or otherwise; it was an arresting phenomenon for a naval officer to compose anything more literary than a logbook entry or an official report.

In the winter of 1825–26, Slidell, tarrying in Madrid with his longing for publication still thwarted, met a man qualified and willing to be his critic and editor. Washington Irving was in the Spanish capital, ostensibly as an attaché to the American ministry, actually to do research for his life of Columbus. The older man sympathized with the younger's ambition, was generous with encouragement and practical suggestion, and gave the aspirant his first appearance in print.

Slidell was permitted to write for the appendix to the Columbus book what Irving was pleased to call in the revised, 1850 edition, *"a very masterly paper"* on the route of the discoverer. Later, the kindly author was largely responsible for bringing his protégé's first book into being. The script for *A Year in Spain, by a Young American,* was edited by Washington Irving, himself. He extended his benevolence by finding Slidell a British publisher.

The book was issued in Boston in 1829, in London, in 1831. From that city, February 22, 1831, Irving wrote to his brother Ebenezer:

"I send a copy of Slidell's 'A Year in Spain' which I corrected for the press and got Murray to publish in very creditable style. It will give the lieutenant a complete launch in literature."

The book was a success both in America and England. Young Slidell, finding himself mildly famous, immediately got to work on another script. This also was to be a travel book: *The American in England*. His published works were factual, save for portions of his later and numerous written justifications of the hangings he had decreed.

The lieutenant from 1830 to 1833 was attached to the frigate *Brandywine* of the Mediterranean Squadron and his professional duties were not severe. They gave him time to write the articles on "Ship," "Navy," and "Navigation" for the *Encyclopedia Americana*, which were published separately in 1833 under the title *Popular Essays on Naval Subjects*, and to get on with *The American in England*. He trusted that when it was completed Mr. Irving again would be co-operative.

There were limits, however, to the patience of a mellow man. Washington Irving had launched Alexander Slidell in literature, but he had no inclination to sign on as his debtor's permanent pilot. He had work of his own to do. From London, where he was completing his *Alhambra*, he wrote to his nephew, Pierre Irving, who had shipped him Slidell's new manuscript:

"Had the Ms been sent to me early last year when I wrote for it, I might have had leisure to prepare it for the press and an opportunity to make a good bargain for it, but when it arrived, every moment and mood that I could devote to literature was completely engrossed. . . . Besides thus leaving no leisure to attend to the correcting of the manuscript of Mr. Slidell, there is no longer a favorable opening for the publication of the work."

The American in England was published in 1835 without Mr. Irving's ministrations. It was less successful than *A Year in Spain*, but its author was not dismayed, nor did his industry abate. He continued to write, despite distractions that in the years immediately ahead were plentiful. Alexander Slidell married Catherine Alexander Robinson of New York on October 1, 1835. He cruised to Russia on the frigate *Independence*, 1837–38, and captained the schooner *Dolphin* in Brazilian waters, 1838–39. In 1841, he was promoted to commander and assigned to the steam sloop, *Missouri*, remaining there until he took over the new brig *Somers*, early in 1842.

Since his rise to independent command was comparatively rapid, Mackenzie must have been a more than satisfactory subordinate, a diligent and scrupulous officer whose probity, if at times irksome, made him unfailingly reliable. His attention to detail unburdened superiors' shoulders.

Men so organized are not always most successful when in complete authority, and the sailor-author, after he began to get vessels of his own, made an unusual captain. He was prim and given to subjecting his crews to long moral lectures. It pleased him to display an elaborate benevolence toward his inferiors, but he employed the cat-o'-nine-tails liberally and its junior flogging instrument, the colt.

His own intense rectitude made him prone to magnify and overpunish trifling misdeeds. This severity was hardly compensated for, in the eyes of the beaten, by the delicacies their captain occasionally sent to the forecastle. One of his adherents testified at Mackenzie's court-martial:

"The treatment of the crew was very humane. I have frequently seen him send dishes from his own table to the sick. I have known him to give fruit from his own private stores to the crew."

The commander was a forerunner of W. S. Gilbert's Captain Reece in his paternal concern for his underlings' welfare:

"Did they with thirst in summer burn?
Lo seltzogenes at every turn
And, on all very sultry days,
Cream ices, handed round on trays."

Mackenzie was precise and sensitively aware of his own rank. It is doubtful whether, despite his solicitude for the morals and welfare of all hands, he was generally popular with them, but he could have assumed command of the *Mantelpiece* or the *Pinafore* with little adjustment, and in Sir Joseph Porter, K.C.B., he would have found a spiritual brother.

During active service and on the leaves he could afford more frequently after he had changed his name, the sailor-author wrote *Spain Revisited*, published in 1836, and in 1841 brought out two two-volume biographies: *The Life of John Paul Jones* and *The Life of Commodore Perry*. *A Year in Spain* continued to be his most popular work.

Mackenzie's books were typical of their period. Minimum progress resulted from every paragraph, and the elegance of each thought was indicated by the number of words attending it. His volumes of travel concerned themselves, in obedience to the taste of a stay-at-home public, with all aspects of the countries traversed—historical, scenic, geographical, archaeological, and sociological. In the biographies he wrote, the subjects were heroic, and his respect for them, absolute.

By modern standards, his books are tedious and cluttered with edifying reflections, yet now and then chinks in the literary façade afford glimpses of a being who was less than the captain of the *Somers* pretended to be and, no doubt, believed he was. Only an immensely self-important and humorless man would have set down these involuntary disclosures.

While he was traveling through Valencia, the diligence that bore young Mr. Slidell and others was held up by three bandits who, before they were driven off by the police, beat in the conductor's head with a rock and, after stunning the postilion, repeatedly knifed him. Among the cowed passengers, none, by his own report, was more abject than the man who, during the *Somers* affair, resented vehemently the least slur upon his courage.

Slidell's companions in the diligence looked away from the horror, but he wrote that his own *"eyes seemed spellbound"* and his ears were *"more sensible than ever."*

"Though the windows at the front and sides were closed, I could distinctly hear each stroke of the murderous knife as it entered its victim. It was not a blunt sound, as of a weapon that meets with positive resistance, but a hissing sound as if the household implement, made to part the bread of peace, performed unwillingly its task of treachery.

"This moment was the unhappiest of my life and it struck me at the time that if any situation could be more worthy of pity than to die the dog's death of poor Pepe, it was to witness his fate, without the power to help him."

Many witnesses to the executions aboard the U.S.S. *Somers*, December 1, 1842, may have known a similarly helpless pity. Alexander Slidell Mackenzie was not among them.

During his Spanish tour, he attended a public hanging in Madrid. The sensations of the man who eighteen years later was to decree and make all the arrangements for a similar execution are worth recording. He found the hangman's pride in his deft accomplishment of his task *"a dreadful propensity of our nature which often leads us to exult in the vilest deed, provided it be adroitly executed,"* and pursued:

"Surely there can be nothing in such a spectacle to promote

morality; nothing to make us either better or happier—a spectacle which serves but to create despondency and array man in enmity with his condition."

The commander had changed his opinion radically by 1842, or else by then his self-righteousness had become impenetrable.

Mr. Irving may have resumed his role of mentor to Mackenzie in later years. The elder author had returned from Europe and had moved into his serene, river-edge home, "Sunnyside," in 1839. During that same year, his former pupil, now Alexander Slidell Mackenzie and well-rewarded for the transformation, bought a farm a few miles north of his late preceptor's residence.

The hillside farmhouse overlooked the Tappan Zee. The commander's friend, Colonel Webb, had a vast stone mansion nearby, later the home of John C. Frémont. All trace of the Mackenzie establishment has vanished, but "Pokahoe," too massively built to fall down, recently has been partly demolished and its remaining first floor transformed into a ranch-house dwelling.

The commander had additional neighbors of distinction. His brother-in-law, Matthew Calbraith Perry; George Morgan, uncle to J. Pierpont Morgan; and Moses H. Grinnell, member of the firm that owned the *Flying Cloud* and other great clipper ships, had summer homes nearby, and at Mr. Irving's "Sunnyside," men of literary fame were forever coming and going.

The commander's admission into the society of important persons inflated an aspiring nature. The sailor-author dedicated his *Spain Revisited* to Lieutenant George P. Upshur, his close friend in the service, who, unless he was as humorless as

Mackenzie, could not have been entirely pleased. That dedication began:

"The chief advantage of the slight reputation that has fallen to my share has been its procuring me the favor and acquaintance of some distinguished individuals whose names might furnish a decoration to my pages which the world would, perhaps, more highly value."

Nevertheless, despite temptations to publicize his new and more exalted friendships, the commander was inscribing his book to his old and, by inference, humbler intimate. George Upshur was brother to Abel P. Upshur, secretary of the navy during the *Somers* scandal, a fact of some significance.

An honor even more substantial than the favor and acquaintanceship of some distinguished individuals was accorded Mackenzie in 1839 by the United States Navy. The unprecedented flowering of one of its officers into a popular author had flustered, then astounded the service, and finally had made it proud. Naval authority paid its tribute to the lieutenant's genius in an order issued June 10, prescribing the *"books to be furnished Vessels of War when on a cruise."*

The list included, along with such literary monuments as the Bible, Shakespeare, Plutarch, Gibbon's *Decline and Fall*, Bowditch's *Navigation*, and Bancroft's *History of the United States, A Year in Spain*, by Alexander Slidell Mackenzie.

The commander's accomplishments as an author exceeded his achievements as an officer and in his time of extremity did much to avert dismissal from the service. Other literary men, not including Mr. Cooper, rushed into print on his behalf. In his own defense, Mackenzie plied his pen with frantic vigor, writing, beside his first official report and its revision and re-revision, coveys of papers addressed to the court of inquiry and then to the court-martial, explaining, protesting, justifying.

Like the cuttlefish, he protected himself by releasing blasts of ink.

Alexander Slidell Mackenzie might have died as he had lived until 1842: an officer of moderate attainments and a writer of some contemporary importance, if fate or coincidence had not interfered. He might have alternated undistinguished service to his profession with leaves spent on the farm his Mackenzie uncle's money had gained him, writing his books and supervising his family, his pigs and cows and gardens.

He would have been remembered then, and only briefly, as a pedantic, pompous man, subject to spells of moralizing, who dearly loved to bask in the favor and acquaintance of the distinguished individuals his neighbor, Mr. Irving, drew about him.

If John Canfield Spencer, secretary of war, had not pushed his son into the navy as a last, despairing means of disciplining him, Mackenzie would have been spared great notoriety, torment, and spiritual exposure.

A mad conjunction of incidents and accidents dragged the commander toward destruction and drove him to write in self-defense papers that disclosed, indirectly yet vividly, the conflicting ruthlessness and timidity, piety and brutality that his surface nature had hidden, perhaps even from himself.

John Canfield Spencer, son of Ambrose, who had been chief justice of the New York Supreme Court and mayor of Albany, was an imperious man, a hard, self-seeking operator who made few friends. His son, Philip, was not among them.

In a time when political fidelity stood on the same moral plane as marital, and was rather more frequently maintained, John Canfield Spencer ruthlessly broke the hallowed bonds of party loyalty whenever a rupture would profit him. Such perfidy, in an age of overheated civic passions, would have ruined a less righteous and able man at once. Spencer smiled grimly at the enemies he made and climbed further.

As a Democrat, he served a term as United States representative and while in office denounced the national bank that, with equal fervor, he later supported. He fished in waters troubled by the disappearance of William Morgan, exposer of Masonry, and became a leader in the short-lived Anti-Masonic Party. As a Whig, he was New York's secretary of state during the administration of William H. Seward, but when all respectable party members denounced Tyler as a traitor, Spencer was entirely willing to become his secretary of war despite ensuing defamation by the orthodox.

He was a lean, sour man with a long face, bitter mouth, and *"fierce, quick-rolling eyes."* His temper was caustic, and he seemed careless of popular praise or blame. This immunity did not cover him against the passive defiance of his own son. The slovenly boy and the ambitious father had little in common beside their surname and mutual antagonism. Rebel himself in a more rewarding fashion, the elder Spencer had no patience with or understanding of Philip's defiance of authority.

Public opinion is a pendulum that, thrust too far in one direction, swings abnormally toward the other. When Commander Mackenzie's story of the hangings aboard his brig was first printed, obliging newspapers attributed to the principal victim all the sins prohibited by the Decalogue, plus supplementary. Philip Spencer, they assured their readers, was a degenerate young monster who had polluted the atmosphere of two colleges until he had been dismissed from each in dark disgrace, a fiend so precociously evil that the world had been freshened by his removal.

When belated investigation proved that these accusations

had been a large overstatement, the pendulum swept back an equal distance from the truth. The public discarded its original beliefs and accepted contrary misinformation. Philip Spencer, lately a deep-dyed scoundrel, was mourned as a bright and innocent lad whom a naval tyrant had put to death for a crime that had never entered the victim's mind. Nothing was done to fortify this contention with competent evidence.

The only known picture of young Spencer is a profile head and shoulders of a homely boy in naval uniform, with a thick shock of hair, heavy eyebrows, and a nose too large for his face. The artist gave his subject the aspect neither of villain nor of paragon, an example that in subsequent years few persons imitated. The profile pose may have been chosen to hide the boy's disfigured eye.

That defect may well have been related to the *Somers* tragedy itself. Philip Spencer had been born with a cast, and for most of his short life nothing effective was done to remedy it. The affliction could not have failed to influence—perhaps it was the principal force that created—the moody, inward-turning nature that ignored obligations, clung to fantasy, and drove a choleric father into recurrent rages. These did not reform his son but pushed him further into his own protective dream world, peopled with swashbucklers and freebooters—romantically lawless beings, drawn from the trashy fiction the boy read avidly.

Philip Spencer must have been less the dolt than his parent deemed him. He was a constant affliction to his instructors, but though he discouraged friendships, his classmates were more amused than irked by him, and at least one distinguished elder saw in him none of the diabolical traits Mackenzie detected.

When news of the *Somers* executions came to William H.

Seward toward the end of his term as New York's governor, he suspended his packing long enough to write from Albany to his wife:

"You have read all that has transpired concerning the awful calamity that has befallen Spencer. Was ever a blow more appalling? I, of course, knew Philip only as friends know our children. I should as soon have expected a deer to ravage a sheep-fold."

Mr. Seward's comparison was strained. There was little of a deer's light grace in the appearance or record of the cross-eyed young rebel.

The tragedy that destroyed the boy and two others was in part of his own making. It was brought about largely by his stupidity, sloth, and insubordination, though with a good deal of help from Alexander Slidell Mackenzie. The death of the young and defenseless inevitably ennobles the victim. The hanging of Philip Spencer has adorned his memory with a forlorn poetic quality that his actual person lacked.

In the fall of 1838, the elder Spencer enrolled his scapegrace son, who was not yet fifteen, at Geneva, now Hobart, College. In the spring of 1841, Philip was withdrawn by his overtried parent. During his more than two years' exposure to education his behavior had been astonishingly consistent. He was still at the foot of the freshman class, the third such body that had harbored him.

Young Spencer's removal had the hearty approval of the college faculty. This was considered by the uninformed in 1842 as proof of the boy's debauched character. In truth, the moral record of the no-account, who apparently had been entirely willing to remain permanently at Geneva, was singularly clean.

During his lengthy residence, the authorities had been obliged to discipline him only twice.

On February 21, 1840, Philip was punished for going home without faculty permission. On November 23, of the same year, he was cited, a shade more gaudily, for embroilment in a cider party that students held to celebrate the election of Harrison and Tyler. Charles D. Vail, who was at Geneva in Spencer's time, described this revel:

"Some fourteen or fifteen students, among them Spencer, had a barrel of cider in one of the rooms and were holding a Whig merrymaking with shouting and singing. Subsequently, by a resolution, some of the participants were pronounced guilty of misconduct."

The boy seems to have taken no conspicuous part in the celebration, although later he did become a drinker. His addiction to liquor was the only certainly proven vice of the many Mackenzie attributed to him, but there is no evidence that he acquired it before joining the navy.

While young Spencer resisted education, he took so slight a part in student activities that men who had been in college in his time could remember in later years little about him save that he was gloomy, kept to himself, was perpetually in trouble with the exigent father, and devoured blood-and-thunder novels. He knew a little Greek and played fairly well on the violin.

In the occasional flashes of activity that enlivened him, Philip Spencer was an effective public speaker. Such outbursts of energy were too brief to impress his instructors and always were followed by a relapse into brooding lethargy. His contemporaries could remember only one instance when he displayed a measure of gaiety.

E. J. Burrall recalled how the college dolt attached himself to the tail of an academic procession and, unobserved by its legitimate members, marched along behind them across the campus, wearing a tall dunce cap with a long streamer, emblazoned: "Patriarch of the Freshman Class."

The apparently permanent freshman, however mentally immature, had a precocious gravity, possibly a by-product of chronic depression, which another classmate, Paul F. Cooper, recollected forty-odd years later.

"I think Spencer's manner must have been remarkable or it would not have made the lasting impression that it has upon my memory. I recall it as more like that of a high-bred man of the world than a boy, just growing into manhood—something very different from the imitation of the manner of older men that is common enough among youngsters."

The incorrigible had more solid substance than his achievements, or lack of them, indicated; for, while at Geneva, he submitted to an operation to adjust his crooked eye. Though warned that the physical and mental anguish would be extreme, Philip Spencer refused to be tied to the table, after the surgical practice of the time, but, lying unrestrained, endured the ordeal with admirable stolidity. Though his vision was bettered, the eye remained faintly askew, giving him the leer that Mackenzie and others were to find indicative of evil.

The boy's improved appearance did not alter his nature. The original disfigurement, his consequent morbidity, and his father's ceaseless hammering had molded his character beyond easy amendment. By the time Philip Spencer left Geneva, he already in essence had become the person whom his commander was to find it imperative to hang. An interview he had with a fellow student, I. H. McCullom, foreshadowed the tragedy:

"I found him in bed, greatly depressed, yet feeling indignant and bitter toward his father on account of his severe reproof which latter, Philip told me, was that unless he turned over a new leaf and did better in the future than he had in the past, he would disown him.

"Brooding over this, he had planned to leave college, go West, change his name, turn land pirate, freebooter or buccaneer on the Mississippi River. These plans were the outgrowth of the kind of reading he had indulged in."

The official minutes of the Geneva College faculty for April 21, 1841, entirely contradict the persistent charge that young Spencer was expelled from the institution for moral delinquencies. The notation read:

"Philip Spencer at the request of his father received a dismission from college. The request was made in consequence of his continued neglect of college exercises and this neglect stated in the letter of dismission; but inasmuch as a change in association might prove favorable, it was also stated that the faculty of this college would make no objection on account of his deficient standing here to his immediate reception in any other college. He was subject to college censure on no other account than the neglect of college exercises."

There could have been small trace of whitewash in this absolution, since Union College immediately accepted the boy as a student, and during his sojourn there, he became one of the founders of Chi Psi fraternity, thereby winning a localized immortality that ignored both his nature and the manner of his death.

The morose rebel has been transformed, by revisers of the fraternity's original ritual, into a tutelary "Saint Philip." Legend, more inaccurate than most, has been woven about his memory for the edification of initiates. A Chi Psi song begins:

> *"Oh here's to Philip Spencer*
> *Who when about to die*
> *When sinking down beneath the wave*
> *Loud shouted out: 'Chi Psi!'*
> *So fill your glasses to the brim*
> *And drink with manly pride.*
> *Humanity received a loss*
> *When Philip Spencer died."*

Philip Spencer's stay at Union was brief. For some further obscure offense, his father, turning in extremity to the then last resort of thwarted parents, obtained an appointment for his son as acting midshipman in the United States Navy.

The navy, since the War of 1812, had relapsed into the stagnation that repeatedly has afflicted the defenses of a people who have wrongly identified each interval between wars as the millennial dawn. The service was top-heavy with men who were distinguished chiefly for their conversatism and longevity. They opposed reform, refused to resign or die, and thereby had dammed the never torrential stream of promotion.

The sorely tried Secretary of War had considered getting his passively mutinous son a commission in the dragoons. Since they were posted on the western frontier, Philip, if assigned to them, would become a less immediate irritation to his father.

Nevertheless, empty land about the boy might be a continual inducement for him to desert. It might be better to send him to sea. In the navy, there would be fewer opportunities for a scapegrace to run away. And this could be said for that service: whatever else it lacked, it still imposed stiff discipline. It taught rebellious youngsters respect and obedience, if little else.

Furthermore, John Canfield Spencer had learned from his

colleague, Secretary Upshur, that young men in the navy would enjoy hereafter greater advantages than they had in the past. If Philip were to change himself radically, a sea career might be the making of him.

Reforms in the service were deliberately under way. Even brassbound authority had become aware that all was not well. The golden age of American ocean commerce had been drawing the nation's best sailors into the merchant marine. Something had to be done—not too much, but something.

Schools already had been established ashore in New York, Boston, and Norfolk, where midshipmen were to be taught those requisites of their profession not easily learned at sea. Venturing further into novelty, the department was dedicating certain vessels to the training of apprentices by the navy and for the navy.

The new brig *Somers* was among these craft, and one of the service's most cultured members had been appointed headmaster of what would be a floating academy, crammed with pupils. Selected officers, commissioned and petty, were to be Commander Mackenzie's faculty.

There is nothing to show whether Philip Spencer welcomed this last of the paternal plans for his rehabilitation. His service record does not indicate that his conduct as an acting midshipman was an improvement over his behavior at Geneva or Union. The fates did not guide him at once into the association that was to destroy him and two intimates.

Acting Midshipman Spencer was assigned to the receiving ship *North Carolina* at the Brooklyn Navy Yard, November 20, 1841, and to the sloop *John Adams*, February 7, 1842. He served on her with the Brazilian Squadron and managed to drink enough to rouse his superiors' disapproval. He was returned to New York, with reputation once more beclouded, on the frigate *Potomac*, July 31, 1842.

The boy's intemperance could not have been heinous, for, at the instance of his commanding officer and possibly through further intervention by his father, he was restored to his rank by Secretary Upshur and was attached to the school brig *Somers* on August 13.

Believers in that number's baleful influence may find the following of interest: The *Somers* sailed on her tragic cruise on September 13. The accomplices listed by Spencer as involved, or likely to be involved, in his plan for mutiny were thirteen. Thirteen witnesses appeared before the impromptu court that condemned Spencer and his comrades to be hanged. Until the boy's death, there were thirteen officers aboard the brig. There were thirteen letters in Philip Spencer's name.

Influences more potent, if even less credible, were to bring about the death of the boy and his principal associates.

CHAPTER 3

Prelude

*"I wish, however, to have nothing to do with baseness in
any shape. The navy is not the place for it."*—ALEXANDER
SLIDELL MACKENZIE.

THE CAPTAIN of the *Somers,* by his own admission, began
to dislike Philip Spencer within an hour of their first meeting,
and the glowering boy soon learned to detest his commander
at least as much. Friction bred by the necessary association of
two wholly antipathetic natures furtively advanced the eventually deadly conflict.

Hatred and the strange terror it bred were the principal
compulsions that finally caused Alexander Slidell Mackenzie
to decree the execution of three men. There were other circumstances, accidents, influences, some of them plainly identifiable, some of them darkly defying definition, which expedited
the triple hanging. One by one, they dropped into place to
form the tragic pattern. Among these precipitating factors, the
Somers, herself, may not have been the least.

The brig-of-war was not to serve merely as a stage and a gallows. She was to supply her particular contribution to a volatile
accumulation that built up at last into frightful explosion.

The vessel was still a slick, new craft when Philip Spencer
first saw her. Built in the Brooklyn Navy Yard, she had been
released from riggers and outfitters for only a few months, and

Mackenzie had just brought her back from her shakedown cruise to the West Indies.

The *Somers* was slim, flush-decked, designed for speed. She was pierced for twelve thirty-two-pound carronades but carried only ten. With a full battery, she had proved dangerously top-heavy and, even with her lighter armament, was cranky. Low in the water, 103 feet overall, 25 at the beam, and displacing 266 tons, she was fleet as the wind and as untrustworthy. She had a faintly baleful arrogance, a vaguely sinister air that, on August 13, 1842, may have caused a young man in a not-too-spruce midshipman's uniform to pause, as he approached her, and stand staring.

The brig's keen hull ran up and outward into a long bow-sprit like a thrust sword, and her masts slanted rakishly across the summer sky. She was not squarely built, like the *John Adams*, or duck-hulled like the *Potomac*. She did not resemble, with her daring, dashing outline, any vessel of war. What a slaver she would make! What a pirate craft!

If such a thought did not occur to Philip Spencer when he first saw the *Somers*, he was to brood on it with increasing frequency in the weeks ahead.

Now he squared his shoulders and strode forward, followed by a porter who trundled the midshipman's dunnage on a wheelbarrow. Ahead of young Spencer was still another ordeal, imposed on him by an unreasonable father. Philip's ears were still ringing with parental commands and warnings. This was his final opportunity to redeem himself; this was his last chance. Influence alone had saved him from being thrown out of the navy in disgrace. John Canfield Spencer would not intervene again.

The boy paused at the pier's edge and looked down on the *Somers'* swarming deck. More men and boys were busy there than he had imagined a vessel of her size could hold. They were coiling ropes, polishing brasswork, manning a sling that lowered supplies through an open hatch. A giant of a man whose red face was enclosed by thick black parentheses of side whiskers was bellowing at a knot of apprentices and threatening to skin them all.

Spencer had seen all this before. Here was the familiar, dreary activity—the reminiscent and, for some reason, faintly sickening tumult. He was back in the navy, whether he liked it or not.

He sighed. More of the same, always more of the same! The brig might look romantic, but she would offer him nothing more than the old, revolting routine. Why didn't he quit? Why didn't he cut and run for it? Why didn't he go—? But he could not imagine where he could go that would be beyond the reach of his father. The boy shrugged again and went aboard his final earthly residence and scaffold. He saluted the flag at the brig's stern and gave his name to the officer of the deck.

A red-haired man with a faintly sanctimonious face laid aside the speaking trumpet that had amplified his orders to the working parties, returned Philip's salute, then smiled and held out his hand.

"Glad to have you aboard, sir," Commander Mackenzie said with moderate warmth. He accepted the newcomer's papers and, turning, bade a midshipman take Mr. Spencer to the steerage and show him where to stow his gear. The boy's guide opened a hatch at the fore end of the trunk that ran lengthwise along the quarter-deck and was raised two feet above it, and led him down into a chamber, four feet wide by fourteen long.

The quarters seemed small, and Spencer said so. He learned the entire brig was overcrowded. She had been designed for a crew of 90; she had 120 men and boys aboard. As for the steerage, where the junior officers were berthed, it was supposed to hold no more than five youngsters and already was occupied by six. With a seventh added, existence there would be unbearably cramped.

Spencer crammed his belongings into the narrow space allotted him and went sullenly back on deck. The old depression had taken hold of him again. Already he felt unwelcome and resented.

A tarry little man, shambling by, looked toward him and tentatively grinned. Spencer smiled back and felt better. If, as heretofore, he was to get no sympathy from his superiors or friendship from his equals, he once again might be able to find relaxation and amusement among members of the crew. There were enough of them, certainly, for him to pick and choose his intimates.

Mackenzie sat at his cabin desk with a scowl marring his usual complacency and his new officer's papers spread before him. Authority had used the commander outrageously by assigning Acting Midshipman Spencer to the *Somers*. This was a school ship, and the young minds aboard her must be protected from moral contamination. Unless Mackenzie could get rid of his new officer, the gentlemen of the steerage would be obliged to mess with a precocious wastrel, a proven drunkard.

The commander would have to move carefully, for, after all, Philip Spencer was the son of the Secretary of War. That made no difference, Mackenzie told himself, glowing with righteousness. The young man's exalted connections only enhanced his own baseness.

"*I beg*," the *Somers*' captain later was to inform the Secretary of the Navy, "*that I may not be misunderstood. I revere authority. I recognize in the exercise of its highest functions in this free country the evidence of genius, intelligence and virtue* [sic] *but I have no respect for the base son of an honored father. On the contrary, I consider that he who by misconduct sullies the luster of an honorable name is more culpable than the unfriended individual whose disgrace falls only on himself.*

"*I wish, however,*" Commander Mackenzie pursued, putting his syntax on straighter, "*to have nothing to do with baseness in any shape. The navy is not the place for it.*"

Philip Spencer, newly arrived, was on his way out again if his captain could manage it. Mackenzie did his best in his protest to his superiors, but they were reprehensibly unimpressed by the threat that an acting midshipman constituted to the purity of the brig, her company, and her commander himself.

Commodore Perry was indifferent to his brother-in-law's objections. And if he wouldn't act, who would? The commodore had two sons aboard the *Somers*. Matthew Calbraith, Junior, was her sailing master; Oliver Hazard was serving as Mackenzie's clerk with temporary midshipman rank. Their father took a dim view of their possible degradation and refused to transfer the base young man.

So, he remained, certified as a suspect member of her company, an added discomfort to the packed-in occupants of the steerage, a threat in his captain's estimation to his subordinates' morals. Spencer made no attempt to increase his popularity with his messmates. If he had, it would have been effort misspent. All the steerage personnel but him were Mackenzie henchmen.

Oliver H. Perry was the commander's nephew. Acting Midshipman Adrien Deslonde was related by marriage to John Slidell of Louisiana, Mackenzie's brother. The remaining midshipmen, less Spencer, had been entrusted by their families to their captain's *"special care."*

Barred from this cohesively loyal group, Philip stood, as heretofore, resentful, defiant, and alone. He could not have been an agreeable associate. He was surly, slovenly, and displayed toward his messmates a maddening air of superior worldly wisdom. Furthermore, he shocked them speechless by his profane estimates of the manners, morals, and intelligence of the *Somers'* captain and, marking their consternation, made his strictures more heinous still.

The boy was not quite suicidal enough to flaunt his growing detestation in the face of the commander himself. In the presence of Mackenzie, he seems to have been outwardly respectful and obedient, if careless in executing orders and dilatory in doing the written exercises assigned to the midshipmen each day to improve them in their profession.

The loose-mouthed young rebel never considered that opinions, rashly voiced in the steerage to ease his own resentment and scandalize his messmates, might be carried aft to the cabin of the captain of the *Somers* by his kin and the young men entrusted to his special care.

In the weeks that elapsed between the time Spencer joined the brig and the day she sailed on her tragic cruise, the boy made no friendships with equals or superiors. Toward the officers intermediate between midshipmen and captain, he seems to have been inoffensive. As the days passed, their persons became more familiar to him, and they assumed three-dimensional identities.

The occupants of the wardroom, situated aft of the steerage, included the second-in-command, Lieutenant Gansevoort, an eager echo of his captain's every opinion; Purser H. M. Heiskill, a devious and slippery individual; Sailing Master Perry; and

Passed Assistant Surgeon—the old navy evolved weird titles—Richard W. Leecock.

Young Dr. Leecock was a Virginian. Sensitive, fair-minded, and still suffering from the aftermath of a bout with yellow fever, he was less fit than his roommates to endure the still unperceived ordeal ahead of them all.

Midway between the midshipmen and the enlisted personnel of the *Somers*, yet belonging to neither category, was a fat young man who bore the title of purser's steward. James W. Wales held an equivocal position and was by nature a dubious person. He was not an officer; he was not a bluejacket; a little above the occupants of the forecastle, who had derisively dubbed him "Whales," yet still below the dwellers in the steerage, Wales's place in the *Somers*' chain of command was negligible and probably, at best, would have been irksome to a slick operator, intent on bettering himself.

His situation at this time was particularly precarious. Efforts of his to improve his condition had backfired to his detriment. He had joined the brig when she had been commissioned. A swindle he had attempted during her maiden cruise had been discovered by Mackenzie, the scourge of all baseness, and Wales had very nearly lost his berth. Why he had not, why, after promises of dismissal, he had been permitted to continue as purser's steward, never will be determined.

The commander, when under fire for the three hangings, referred coyly to the trouble between him and Wales as *"a misunderstanding."* The purser's steward, when asked about it, refused to say anything, but his reticence did not hide permanently the nature of his offense, thanks to George Warner, that feeble mutineer. My great-uncle wrote:

" *'Whales,' the purser's steward had a difficulty at St. John's, Porto Rico, with parties who claimed he had cheated them, or rather, intended to pay, as they say on shipboard, with the fore-topsail, but the matter being reported to the Captain, the sharper was made to settle with the assurance from Captain Mackenzie that, as soon as the vessel arrived in the United States, he (Whales) would be put ashore, as he would have no such disreputable person on the vessel he commanded. On arriving in N. Y., Whales was not put ashore but remained in the capacity of Purser's Steward."*

Whatever inspired the commander's uncharacteristic leniency, he must, in time, have become profoundly grateful for it. Now, while Mackenzie's seagoing seminary prepared for an educational cruise to the West African Coast, Wales, still in disrepute and uncertain of his berth, was taking the best means he knew to restore himself to favor: he was keeping a record of his shipmates' misdeeds and, with ears cocked and eyes wide, was bent on enlarging his collection.

Wales watched Philip Spencer with special care. He could see that Commander Mackenzie did not like his new acting midshipman. Already the purser's steward had gathered here and there incidents to the young man's discredit. Mr. Spencer, it was plain, stood aloof from the gentlemen of the quarter-deck. Mr. Spencer was stooping low to make friends and win popularity. He was slighting his social equals and, contrary to standards of officer conduct, was leveling himself with the crew and becoming especially intimate with two of its members. It might be worth while for Wales to pay still closer attention to this reckless young man.

Whether Philip Spencer was a scoundrel, rebel, fool, delinquent, or a blend of all four, it is possible to sympathize with him in these last months of his life. There scarcely could have been more unpropitious surroundings for the reform of an eighteen-year-old problem boy than the U.S.S. *Somers*. The omens had been dark when he had first boarded her. They were growing blacker.

The boy's nature and background had made his service in the navy a dangerous experiment from its beginning. He was still the sluggish and surly person who had been willing to remain, until his father's patience had run out, patriarch of successive freshman classes. He had not changed, but his situation had altered radically, and in this the hazard lay.

While young Spencer had stagnated in college, he had been disregarded by his associates and had compensated for their indifference by gaudy daydreams beyond possible realization. Transfer from a dormitory to a war vessel had improved his position. He now had authority and rank that hitherto, and fortunately, he had lacked.

On the brig, a hundred-odd enlisted men and boys were supposed to accord Acting Midshipman Spencer obedience and at least surface respect, providing a novel and heady stimulus for a previously neglected boy. To some extent his rank enabled him to implement the fantasies he still indulged in to protect himself from the dislike or, at best, the indifference of his brother officers.

John Canfield Spencer could not have chosen a more risky method of reforming his moody son, nor could any mortal have been found more certain to accelerate the calamity the boy brought down upon himself than Commander Alexander Slidell Mackenzie, U.S.N. The prudish and pompous headmaster of a marine academy was not a person likely to sympathize with, or excuse, the extravagances of a psychically bruised delinquent.

The association of an egocentric prig who possessed unlimited power and a blatant young insurgent who mocked it was mathematically certain to end in trouble, small or great. The initial responsibility for the dreadfulness the next three months were to bring forth rests upon Philip Spencer. His was the first impulse that, gathering momentum, destroyed him and his closest friends.

James W. Wales watched quietly yet intently the waxing intimacy between a young gentleman of the steerage and two enlisted hands. The purser's steward already had acquired a deal of general, and possibly negotiable, material by observing the unofficerlike attitude of Spencer toward the whole crew. He joked with the men and cut antics for the boys to make them laugh, invited the apprentices to scramble for coins he cast on the deck, gave tobacco to young and old. Sometimes he threw his audience into raptures by dislocating his own jaw and, *"by contact of the bones"* producing tunes *"with accuracy and elegance."*

This clowning before inferiors, this spendthrift generosity toward seamen and apprentices, ill became an officer, but Spencer's antics were performed too publicly for Wales to gain greatly by reporting them. The young man's intimacy with Samuel Cromwell and Elisha Small could yield a larger profit. Spencer in his spare time was continually in close conversation with one or the other of his new cronies. Upon these conferences, the purser's steward spied and eavesdropped assiduously.

Many of the factors, physical and spiritual, that brought about the execution of Philip Spencer are discernible. It is more difficult to picture the men who died with him as authentic accomplices in a veritable plan for mutiny.

Though Mackenzie, in a belated effort to justify his hanging of Cromwell, even submitted the man's corpse to grisly investigation, little that is definite is known of his past beyond the facts that he lately had married and, before that, had come up the hard way to a rating of boatswain's mate.

It was whispered aboard the *Somers* that Cromwell had been pirate and slave runner. It also was said, more provably, that he was a bully, a blusterer, and an insubordinate ranter.

Cromwell was the largest man aboard the *Somers*—tall, burly, with whiskers split by a shaven chin—a good seaman with some knowledge of navigation. His bellowing rages scared the wits out of the apprentices, frightened his equals, and awed his superiors. They, too, were afraid of him. Still Mackenzie had advanced him to the rating of acting boatswain.

In a vessel where discipline was more sternly imposed, any one of Cromwell's recurrent outbursts would have won him at least a flogging. Until that still-imperceptible crime that led to his hanging, he was never punished for his defiances of discipline. The logbook of the brig said so.

The man told Gansevoort to his face that an order the lieutenant issued was *"damned hard usage."* He took his own sullen time in obeying orders and once, while furling sail, roared to the lieutenant: *"God damn the jib and the lacing and the damned fool that invented it!"*

The inventor of the jib lacing was Alexander Slidell Mackenzie, and Cromwell knew it. Gansevoort *"reproved him severely."*

Nothing more than that. If the acting boatswain dared to God-damn his captain in the presence of that captain's second-in-command, he must have ventured further into insolence with the lesser and singularly spineless officers of the brig. A violent man, Cromwell, a really dangerous man. It was best to let him alone.

The patly named Elisha Small was the least in stature

among the adult company of the brig, a dwarfish man with a
giant's thirst. He, like Cromwell, was an accomplished sailor
and, when Spencer joined the *Somers*, was serving as quarter-
master. Later, he was broken back to seaman for "carelessness
and neglect of duty," possibly a euphemism for drunkenness.

Small had been employed in 1840 as agent for a Salem firm
on the African West Coast; after that, he had been second
mate on the Boston brig, *Angola*. He had lost this post, too,
through drink.

Africa! Slavery! Piracy! Two hard-bitten seamen were more
than willing to tell lurid and probably highly fictional tales
concerning all these to an enthralled, fantastically generous
boy. Before the *Somers*, that raiderlike craft, put to sea, the
pattern of the tragedy was forming.

Slavers, as well as pirates, still were actual beings in the
early 1840's. Prototypes of twentieth-century rumrunners were
still loading black ivory in the West Africa barracoons and
smuggling it into America. Congress had forbidden the slave
trade in 1808. Despite the efforts of British and United States
cruisers, it continued.

So, while the attentive Wales stood nearby with ears cocked,
Cromwell and Small spun their yarns—and indirectly nooses
for their necks. Spencer, unstable imagination afire, paid them
off lavishly in cigars he bought from the purser's slop chest and
brandy he bribed Waltham, the Negro wardroom steward, to
supply.

There was more liquor aboard his vessel, Mackenzie reported to Upshur with the air of a housewife deploring the
cockroaches in the kitchen, than he wished to have on board.
The wardroom officers, their commander explained, had laid
in a store of brandy *"to be used medicinally"* as a remedy for

malaria. By mistake, twice the stipulated quantity had been delivered, a regrettable error in the eyes of the commander, who held *"that the drinking of brandy is even more dreadful than malaria."*

All the liquid dreadfulness, the *Somers'* captain assured the Secretary, was intact aboard the brig, *"except what was stolen by the steward at the request of Mr. Spencer and drank by him and those he endeavored to corrupt."*

Mackenzie was never deterred from moral loftiness by obstructive facts. Brandy was used freely aboard his vessel by others beside Spencer and his beneficiaries.

On September 13, 1842, the brig *Somers* stood out through the Narrows and bowed to the first Atlantic roller. All actors in the gestating tragedy had been gathered aboard her.

There was shouting on the deck and bellowing from the yardarms, where dizzy apprentices wrestled with stiff canvas. One by one, the loftier sails were sheeted home. They filled. The *Somers* slid more swiftly through the waves. She was more instantly responsive, far fleeter, than any craft Philip Spencer had known.

The brig dropped her lee rail still lower. Blithely, she flung the knots behind her. No vessel could overtake this swift, enraptured creature; none could escape her.

The boy looked up at the white towers of wind-spread fabric. What a slaver the *Somers* would be! What a pirate!

CHAPTER 4

Enough Rope

*"Servile in his intercourse with me, when among the crew,
he loaded me with blasphemous vituperations."*—ALEXANDER
SLIDELL MACKENZIE.

WHEN THE last dim land had melted into ocean and the
Somers was well away on her long run to Madeira, her company proceeded to implement the prime purpose of her
voyage: the education of hitherto aspiring, now homesick and
seasick apprentices.

Headmaster Mackenzie, his officer-professors, and seamen-
instructors began the discipline and enlightenment of their
pupils. The boys' lot was not entirely enviable. Mercy seldom
tempered their commander's peculiar sense of justice. Furthermore, their school, with 120 beings housed in space designed
for 90, was miserably overcrowded.

The mutiny that Philip Spencer was hanged for planning
would have been a singularly juvenile revolt. Only six of the
brig's seamen and apprentices were more than nineteen years
old; forty-five were sixteen or less; and three were barely thirteen. The seagoing pupils were an unhappy lot at the beginning of their cruise and, though they had improved in skill
and demeanor by the time the dark voyage had ended, they
had encountered singularly little to cheer them during its
course.

The Mackenzie ocean-borne seminary adhered to the

47

Squeersian school of pedagogy: boys, having been taught a skill with the assistance of a rope end, thereafter were expected to employ it deftly, aloft or below. The apprentices led a painful life, yet their education advanced, beckoned forward by the edifying homilies their captain delivered publicly on all possible occasions, and urged on from behind by lash-wielding instructors. Mackenzie, lord of his little world, chastened far oftener than he cherished.

Floggings were frequent. They varied in duration and in the type of scourge employed with the age of the offender and the nature of his offense. Adults were beaten, not more than twelve lashes by navy law, with the standard, nine-tailed cat. For juvenile evildoers, a lighter model was used, sometimes with several of its cords tied back. On still more trifling sinners, a colt was employed. This was a single-stranded instrument with a lash of little-finger diameter.

Besides the formal punishments that were meted out at morning musters, more impromptu stimulations to proficiency were visited upon the lazy and stupid. Their teachers agreed with the land-bound instructors of that age that a soundly boxed ear quickened its proprietor's perceptions and that a well-placed kick drove intelligence upward.

None of the *Somers'* faculty was tolerant of error, but the terror of the apprentices was the bellowing, bewhiskered Samuel Cromwell. He frightened the youngsters into paroxysms by roaring ghastly predictions of what he would do to them in another moment. After he had hanged Cromwell, Mackenzie remembered that he had reproved the acting boatswain for his brutality.

Intervention by Thomas Dickenson, carpenter's mate, may have saved one Sears, an unproficient apprentice, from slaughter by Cromwell, who, enraged by the boy's stupidity, threw a stick at his head and missed. Thereupon, according to Dickenson:

"He picked up another and swore by God Almighty that he would knock out his brains if he swung from the yard-arm the next minute. I hallooed at him and the boy sank to his knees, expecting his death blow. Cromwell stayed his hand and said to me: 'Your time is damned short.'"

Mackenzie offered this anecdote as an indication that, long before the brig reached Madeira, mutiny was simmering in the acting boatswain's mind. The commander's mental mill accepted a wide diversity of grist.

The *Somers* made her Madeira landfall, tarried briefly at Funchal, then slanted south and east through warmer, bluer seas toward the peaks of drowned mountains that are the Canary Islands. Mackenzie was carrying dispatches for the U.S. Sloop *Vandalia* and hoped to overtake her at Tenerife.

There was no visible sign that mutiny's virus was working aboard the brig unless Philip Spencer's intimate association with his inferiors was indicative. He continued to endear himself to the crew by his friendliness and liberality. Before his end, this generosity had reached massive proportions. The shrewd steward watched with interest while Spencer's indebtedness to the slop chest mounted.

Between September 12 and November 26, the prodigal acting midshipman was debited with ten pounds of tobacco and seven hundred "segars."

The boy was a heavy smoker, but most of his withdrawals must have been handed on to seamen and apprentices. He was, Wales observed, particularly openhanded with the boys—perhaps in simple generosity, perhaps to defy Mackenzie, who frowned upon the use of tobacco by the young.

Spencer's friendship with Cromwell and Small was not diminishing. He still supplied them with cigars and, through his nefarious compact with Waltham, the wardroom steward, got them brandy as well. It was all, Wales decided, very puzzling. He continued to watch.

The true quality of Philip Spencer's association with Samuel Cromwell and Elisha Small never will be determined. The boy may have tried to enlist his intimates in a crack-brained plot. Unquestionably, he did discuss it with Small, who, perhaps in a boozy moment, gave the conspiracy lip endorsement. It is hard to imagine that the hard-boiled Cromwell ever let himself be involved. There is no vestige of proof that he did.

Two veteran, adult seamen, whatever their mental limitations, could not have become genuine accomplices in a fantastic mutiny-to-be planned by an unstable boy with no discernible ability to lead anything—even himself.

There is one presumption that at least makes plausible this otherwise unlikely association that brought three men to death. Is it not possible that two reprehensibly self-seeking sailors identified Spencer, not as a master rebel born to ride and rein the whirlwind, but as a silly boy, bombastic, mentally addled by the romantic swill he had read, yet nevertheless a reliable source of free tobacco and liquor, with occasional extra dividends of cash? Could it not have been that Cromwell and Small humored their benefactor for the sake of favors received and a lively hope of more to come?

"Yes, sir, Mr. Spencer, sir. A great pirate was lost when you joined the navy. Them was fine cigars, Mr. Spencer. Could you favor me with a couple more, sir?"

"Right you are, Mr. Spencer. You could take the brig, easy enough, with a few bold lads like yourself and what, begging your pardon, sir, about a tot of brandy for the cruel pain in my belly?"

Neither Small nor Cromwell could have been aware of danger lurking in their tolerance of the boy and his vaporings. The United States Navy didn't have mutinies. If the practical, and profitable, joke they were perpetrating on Philip Spencer should be uncovered, any normal officer would laugh at it.

Thus, Cromwell and Small may have reasoned. If so, they overlooked the dire fact that the *Somers* was commanded by a peculiar and humorless being and that his officers closely resembled him.

The brig raised the twin peaks of Tenerife, Canary Islands, and anchored off Santa Cruz in late October. The *Vandalia* was still ahead of them. She had paused here but had gone on to Liberia. The *Somers*, her dispatches still undelivered, followed.

Parching winds blew out of Africa. No one who permissibly could stay topside lingered below. Men and boys off watch by preference remained on deck, many of them sleeping there. This congestion expedited the snooping of the greedy James W. Wales.

No one can tell whether the purser's steward already had begun to peddle to his superiors items he had industriously collected. Whether or no, Mackenzie insisted in his report that, after the brig had left Madeira, the discipline of his command rapidly fell to pieces. He offered no instances to support his statement; he just said so, and his officers, as usual, agreed with him although, still imitatively, none supplied specific instances to fortify his contention.

Did the crew refuse to obey orders? Well, no; but they

seemed—slow. Did a single man or boy defy a superior? Not exactly, but they appeared—unwilling.

The commander and his faithful chorus reached too far. All evidence indicates that the men and boys whom they tried to picture as incipient mutineers were extraordinarily patient beings. The crew was still green; it was unwieldy, yet it is doubtful whether any mariners ever bore steadily increasing provocation more docilely.

Furthermore, if Mackenzie's command had been composed largely of shirkers and worse, that would have been principally his own fault. He had been permitted to pick and choose his crew from the unassigned adults and youngsters on the receiving ship *North Carolina*. He had selected them, he said himself, for *"their physical appearance and their indications of health, activity, intelligence and spirit."*

The logbook of the *Somers*, a frequent postexecution embarrassment to Mackenzie, attested that from October 6, when the brig reached Madeira until November 26, when Spencer was arrested, no single member of the brig's crew was cited for disobedience. Men were flogged for theft, for laziness, for fighting among themselves, but not for insubordination.

If discipline indeed fell to pieces, the *Somers'* officers made no recorded attempt to check the deterioration; they listed the punishment of not one insurgent.

The *Somers* reached Liberia on November 10, and anchored off Cape Mesurado, meanly crowned by the colony's ten-year-old capital, Monrovia. The *Vandalia* had been there but had sailed weeks earlier. Mackenzie resolved to break off pursuit and begin his homeward voyage. Before he weighed anchor, he allowed his crew shore leave in the stench and dazzle of the little town. Most of his men returned laden with the useless gadgets sailors are prone to buy, but Purser's Steward Wales brought back a more valuable item. He added it to his collection of Philip Spencer's misdeeds.

The acting midshipman was in command of a cutter that took men ashore, and Wales, by accident or design, was among his passengers. Before the boat pulled away, Mackenzie chewed out Spencer for not being properly uniformed and later shouted after him, demanding whether he had the national flag aboard.

Spencer called back that he had not and then, dropping his voice, informed his passengers:

"And I'll be God-damned if I'll go back for it, either. To hell with the damned old humbug."

He continued to curse the commander until the cutter was beached. Wales was an attentive listener. He was particularly interested to observe that the rest of Spencer's audience seemed more than pleased.

The *Somers* sailed from Monrovia on November 11, to slant northwest across the Atlantic toward St. Thomas, Virgin Islands, where Mackenzie intended to reprovision. The course she followed was glamorous to a reader of romantic trash.

This was the sea road the slave runners traveled. It was easy for the acting midshipman to imagine, when he looked aloft at the raked masts scrawling invisible ellipses upon the brilliant sky, that this fleet vessel was one of an unholy company and Philip Spencer her dashing commander.

On November 16, shining particles appeared on the reeling horizon astern. The officer of the deck leveled his glass. They were the sails of a following vessel, perhaps an actual slaver, perhaps even a pirate.

Mackenzie beat to quarters, rousing a vast, unwarlike confusion. By the time it had been suppressed and small arms had been loaded and served out, the oncoming craft identified herself as a British cruiser. Her suspicions had been aroused by the *Somers'* sinister appearance. Undeceived, she broke off the chase.

Cromwell, while the frenzy had endured, had stood at his station, taking no pains to conceal his vast scorn of the helterskelter running and the officers' confused commands. When the furore had ended, the whiskered giant grinned at the stillagitated Midshipman Charles W. Hays.

"A *damned sight of humbug about nothing*," Cromwell said deliberately. "*I've been on a vessel where shot were fired and not half as much noise about it.*"

The acting boatswain's derision, insubordinate but unpunished, did not abash Philip Spencer. In the babble of men and boys when the crisis was over, no voice was raised more boastfully or recklessly than his. He told what he would have done, had he been in his commander's place, and the observant Wales noted that down, too.

If Spencer's unbalanced behavior was, as Mackenzie came to believe, a prelude to mutiny, no conspirator since the world began more generally advertised his intentions. The purser's steward filed each misdemeanor away for future reference. His subject's conduct rapidly lengthened the baleful record.

The acting midshipman continued, not too surreptitiously, to supply Cromwell and Small with cigars and brandy. He was often seen in confidential talk with one or the other. Wales, one day, was particularly fortunate in his sleuthing, for the suspect displayed a drawing he had made of the brig "*with a black flag flying at her peak.*"

Spencer attained the apogee of indiscretion for a prospective mutineer in a conversation he had with Orderly Sergeant Michael H. Garty, sole marine aboard the brig and serving there as master-at-arms. The boy discussed with the being who was in essence the *Somers'* policeman the most practical way of capturing the vessel. According to Garty, the conversation ran thus:

"*She's a fine craft, the* Somers, *Sergeant.*"

"*She is that, sir.*"

"*All the same, I think I could take her with six men.*"

"*Take her with six men! Indeed no, sir; nor with three times six.*"

"*But I could,*" Spencer insisted. "*First, I'd secure the captain and officers. Then, I'd turn out the crew. When they saw me and my men, armed and ready, I've not a doubt they'd surrender.*"

"*Have you not? You and six men against all of us? Why, sir, we'd rush you and throw you overboard. You could shoot down no more than a half dozen at the most. It's a very poor crew you must consider us if you think you could take us with six men.*"

That is the way the orderly sergeant told it. Mackenzie later was to recommend his promotion to lieutenant in the Marine Corps.

Spencer, in idleness—or lunacy—went still further. After debating with a cop the best way to commit a crime, he was overheard asking Cromwell what sort of a pirate vessel the *Somers* would make. Plunging deeper still into garrulous indiscretion, Spencer told Gansevoort at one time and Garty at another that he soon expected to have a vessel of his own. The master-at-arms heard the boy ask Cromwell how the acting boatswain would like to sail with him.

"*Cromwell said he would like it well. Mr. Spencer said it might make an alteration in him to have command but that Cromwell might not take notice of that.*"

Thus, day by day as the brig rolled homeward, Philip Spencer, babbler, imbecile, or mutineer, boasted and postured. The reckless sound and fury might have signified no more than a slighted youngster's attempt to employ a new version of his old daydreams as a shield against reality. It might even have been madness, divinely visited on one marked for destruction.

His still unaroused audience's implicit opinion of the tiresome braggart was perhaps an accurate diagnosis. To them, Wales excepted, he seemed an endlessly garrulous young man, sometimes amusing, more often a pest. No one paid him more than a faintly long-suffering attention—no one, that is, but the observant purser's steward.

In this general disregard of Spencer, Mackenzie himself had shared. He confessed to Upshur:

"Perhaps I had reproved him less frequently than others for slight deviations from duty. I had little hope of essentially serving one who had been so great an enemy to himself."

Popular indifference toward a manic gabbler did not hush him; instead, it drove him disastrously further. Whatever possessed him—whether it was dementia, childish daydreaming, or a genuine if ridiculous intention to lead a mutiny—blinded him to danger. His minor misbehavior had continued so long unpunished that he presumed to undertake greater.

As though the endless reeling of the brig were shaking his mind loose from all stability or discretion, Spencer voiced to his companions in the steerage still more caustic opinions of the commander and his abilities.

Whether as a result of these comments or other impieties, he was involved a few days before his arrest in a fist fight with Midshipman Egbert Thompson, which, as far as the record indicates, was the most strenuous achievement of Philip Spencer's life. In his more public conduct, he ventured even further in insubordination.

James W. Wales happened—just happened—to be nearby when Mackenzie called his problem subordinate aft and berated him for negligence. When the boy came forward again, he was raging. The working party he had been directing stared at him, and the purser's steward asked ingenuously:

"Why, whatever is the matter?"

Spencer's face was black, his voice shaking.

"The commander," he stormed, "said I did not pay attention to my duty and requested me in the future to do better. God damn him! I'd like to catch him on that roundhouse [the after part of the quarter-deck] some night and plunge him overboard. God damn me if I don't do it, too."

Wales observed that seamen and apprentices within earshot were grinning. He himself smiled for divergent reasons of his own.

Philip Spencer, though hanged for mutiny, more literally talked himself to death.

CHAPTER 5

Cry Havoc

"The mutinous imagining of a single heart, if revealed to a single ear, with a corrupting purpose, brings down upon the offender the death-bearing sentence of the law."—ALEXANDER SLIDELL MACKENZIE.

THE TRADE wind piped in the rigging like a spectral boatswain, and luminous sails scrubbed the pale stars. Shadows upon the *Somers'* deck washed about like black fluid in time to her rolling. The uneven beat of impact and the following crash of spray came aft as the brig's forefoot split the waves. Sea fire streamed from her flanks, and the moon's shattered reflection filled the wake with unearthly brilliance.

It was an hour after the swift tropical nightfall on Friday, November 25, 1842—an eerie hour that magnified each creak and rattle of the *Somers'* passage, a dark and boding time, fit for the disclosure of dreadful secrets.

Two dim figures sat on the booms—the spare spars, piled and secured amidships. Their heads were close; their voices, low. Purser's Steward Wales was receiving unexpected, appalling confidences.

Wales had been standing by the bitts—the ends of a sailing vessel's rib timbers that protrude above the deck—when Philip Spencer, perched upon the booms, had invited the steward to join him.

According to Wales's first report of the conversation, the acting midshipman demanded, *"Whales, do you fear death? Do you fear a dead man? Do you fear to kill a man?"*

Wales squinted suspiciously. The darkness hid Spencer's face, but his voice sounded earnest enough. The purser's steward coughed the sudden dryness from his throat and returned a valiant negative to each question.

"Then," Spencer said hollowly, *"I will bind you with the oath,"* and uttered a bloodcurdling obligation to secrecy that Wales, still wary, repeated. What followed swept away the last of his skepticism, for his companion drew breath and then loosed a fantastic tale that, in the gloom and the whistling wind, was hair-raising as well.

Mutiny was about to explode aboard the *Somers*, and Spencer was ready to fire the charge. He had planned remorselessly and well. With twenty who already had taken the oath he had imposed on Wales, he intended to revolt, take the brig, murder her officers and all loyal men, and turn the *Somers* into a pirate craft.

Wales was shivering, though the night was warm. Fear was uppermost in his devious mind, yet he must already have begun to calculate the value of this intelligence, provided he could live long enough to employ it. Spencer was continuing, still in that hollow, spine-tingling voice:

He and his twenty formidable accomplices were determined to start a fight in mid-watch some night. When the officer of deck interfered, they would overpower him and throw him overboard. This was to be the first of manifold murders. The mutineers were to rush into the cabin and slaughter Commander Mackenzie. Then, Spencer himself would enter the wardroom and deftly kill the officers berthed there.

The wind keened in Wales's ears; the laboring brig groaned funereally. Spencer's awesome delivery was increasing the tale's horror.

He had determined where the keys of the arms chests were kept. When the senior officers had all been exterminated, Spencer would serve out muskets and ammunition to his followers and then call the entire crew up on deck. Those who seemed fitted for a life of piracy would be enlisted. The deficient and unwilling would be drowned.

Spray, flung up by the brig's bows, spattered across the deck, and Wales flinched. Squatting beside Spencer on the booms, quaking at the ghostly sounds that ran through the darkness, the purser's steward had swallowed uncritically all that had been confided, and he downed the remainder without a qualm.

The triumphant mutineers, their future commander was confiding, would sail the *Somers* to Cape San Antonio or the Isle of Pines and there take aboard a veteran pirate, an intimate of one of the conspirators, who would tutor the aspirants in their new profession.

Spencer paused at this point, looked cautiously about him, and then called Small up out of the gloom. They began to talk about something that Wales *"could not exactly understand,"* but, when the dwarfish seaman was reluctant to continue the conversation in the steward's presence, Spencer assured him that Wales was *"one of us,"* and Small, apparently relieved, said he was *"very glad."* He left at this point to obey an order shouted by a watch officer. Spencer called after him that they would talk again later and bade him, meanwhile, to see *"that foretop man."*

The acting midshipman then turned to Wales again and pointed out that Mackenzie had a large amount of money aboard, which, with the purser's fund, would make *"a pretty little sum"* to start them off on their new profession. He then invited Wales to join in the mutiny.

"I did not tell him whether I would, or would not, but rather leaned on his side, in order to obtain further intelligence of their movements."

Everything had been arranged, Spencer confided. The plan for the uprising had been carefully prepared in secret writing and even then was concealed in his own neckerchief. He would show it to Wales later.

Someone sang out for the purser's steward. When he responded, Spencer followed him aft.

"Remember," the acting midshipman growled, *"if you breathe a syllable of what I have communicated, your life won't be worth a straw. You will be murdered, if not by me, by some of those concerned. Escape will be impossible."*

Then, switching from threat to persuasion, he offered Wales the berth of third officer on the pirate brig.

"I told him I would talk to him tomorrow on the subject. Here we parted for the night."

James W. Wales, angling his way aft, past members of the watch and the seamen and apprentices asleep on deck, must have staggered under the weight of his prize. Avarice, succeeding fright, blinded him to numerous implausibilities in Spencer's tale; prevented the purser's steward's even questioning whether just possibly he had not been the victim of a gigantic hoax.

He did not ask himself why Spencer should confide in him, a mere acquaintance; or why he should air his preposterous plot in so exposed a place, with the watch moving about and many idlers lounging on deck; or how the serial massacre of the *Somers'* officers was to be accomplished in silence so complete that the not-yet-murdered would not be aroused.

None of these questions seem to have bothered the purser's steward, then or later. He was far too occupied, this night, in estimating the worth of the astounding information. This priceless addition to the list of Spencer's misdeeds, this collector's item, would clean Wales's besmirched reputation; it would win him reward from a grateful commander. One thing was certain: he must plot his course carefully; he must not endanger his future by raising a premature alarm.

So, the purser's steward, lately apprised of imminent mutiny and wholesale murder, went to his hammock but not to sleep. He had to evaluate, in cash and credit, the calamitous secret confided to him.

Unless Wales was profound, as well as acute, unless he had plumbed the minds of his superiors and become aware of their tinder-dry inflammability, he must have underestimated his new possession. Even if all that Spencer had told him was true, disclosure could only set a subordinate's word in balance against an officer's, though it was an officer whom Mackenzie detested.

It would be well for the informer-to-be, lying wide-eyed in his hammock, to go through his collection of Spencer's defamations of the commander and be ready, at need, to recite them. Wales would require all his wits and courage after he had told his story. Hadn't Spencer warned that betrayal would mean death?

Suppose the acting midshipman and Small should meet the steward's charges with a simple denial that any such episode had occurred? Wales had no witnesses to support him.

The dark brig surged through darker seas with moonlight

following and stars reeling above her while Wales flopped about in his hammock like a netted fish and the three men whom his still-unuttered tale would destroy slept through the first of the six nights remaining to them on earth.

It is reaching far into fantasy to suggest that something hovered above the long fire of the *Somers'* wake—something patient yet baleful, indefinable yet very terrible, something that waited the indicated moment when it would board a United States man-of-war and for five days and nights of demeaning, unmanning, continually growing fear possess her.

The assumption is preposterous, yet is it less so, by any sane measurement, than the ghastly sequence of indecencies and outrages Wales and his still-undisclosed tidings were to launch?

You cannot identify or explain that five-day-long seizure; you can see only its consequences—the successive horrors it wrought. They might more easily be disbelieved if they had not been set down without discernible regret or penitence by those who had committed them.

The baseless apprehensions of the terrified were to inflate a slovenly boy and his silly intention into a menace so monstrous that three human sacrifices had to be offered, lest otherwise the afflicted collapse from fear.

The strange frenzy has been called "the *Somers* mutiny." It might better have been named "the *Somers* terror." James W. Wales sponsored it. How much of his precipitating tale, untold all this shining Friday night, was truth, how much the product of his devious mind, no one can be sure.

This much is provable: the purser's steward was neither an accurate nor even honest reporter.

Wales wrote out, at some time during the following day, his

first version of his talk with Spencer. His second and third narratives were elaborations of the first. Practice improved and expanded each of them. The purser's steward was able to remember, twenty-four days later, a good deal that he did not recall twenty-four hours after the fatal interview. By then, Spencer, Cromwell, and Small had been dead nineteen days.

In his second statement, on December 19, Wales altered his original version of the conversation between the acting midshipman and Small. The purser's steward had said earlier that the two had *"talked about something I could not exactly understand."* Now, he remembers that they had spoken in Spanish, a notoriously piratical language.

The incident of the neckerchief and the plan for the uprising it concealed is enlarged in this second statement and is transposed as well. Wales writes now that it took place, not toward the close of the interview but at its beginning. He also reveals that he had taken hold of the fabric at Spencer's direction and that *"there was a rumpling which showed there was a paper in back of it."*

The steward's new tale maintains that Spencer and others— not the acting midshipman, alone, as in the first version—were to massacre the wardroom officers. Since his earlier statement, Wales also has managed to recollect that the occupants of the steerage were to be murdered, too.

There is further amendment. The reporter now says he was told by Spencer that, after the officers had all been exterminated and before the crew was called up on deck, the two sternmost carronades were to be swung inward to bear upon the company and prevent resistance.

There are further divergences between statements one and two. Wales's oddly deferred total recall has enabled him to present, tardily but completely, the diabolical intentions of Spencer when he should be launched at last upon a piratical career:

"Whenever they took a vessel, after taking from her what would be of use to them, they were to murder all on board and scuttle the vessel so as to leave no trace of her. Should there be any females on board of the vessels they would take, they would have them removed to the brig for the use of the officers and men—using them as long as they should see fit and then making way with them."

The steward, in version two, fixes the duration of the interview for the first time—"nearly two hours." He gives a more definite explanation why he did not report the conspiracy immediately: "I observed that Small was watching me closely." Wales also remembers belatedly that he did try to get through the steerage into the wardroom and spread the alarm, but that Spencer, from his hammock, had demanded "what the devil I was about, cruising around there."

The third and apparently final literary work of James W. Wales was issued on February 6, 1843, seventy-three days after the event. It had fewer divergences from its predecessors, yet an acutely retroactive memory was able to furnish several. The narrator now recalls that Small warned Spencer not to speak so loudly, "saying there were a number of little pitchers about that had long ears—alluding to the boys."

Wales also recollects, for the first time and almost two and a half months after the event, that he waited till next day to report his talk with the master mutineer because, when it had ended and Spencer had turned in, Small followed the steward suspiciously "wherever I went." All the following day, too, he says he was "dogged" by Small and Cromwell.

With his third version completed, Wales laid aside his pen,

to employ it henceforth only for private purposes. Though each of his two later statements had filled in gaps and smoothed out discrepancies in the original and had industriously blackened still further the memory of Philip Spencer, neither was anything more competent than an ex post facto justification of a triple execution.

It was Wales's first story, this lone, unsupported accusation, this, and a sourceless, ghastly frenzy, that destroyed the alleged archmutineer and his so-called accomplices. When Spencer's talk with the purser's steward had ended, the boy had finished his part in the crime that was to swing him and his two friends aloft in grisly companionship.

There was only dubious evidence to warrant the hanging of Philip Spencer, less to involve Small. None that was even remotely competent was ever brought against Samuel Cromwell, who died with them.

The moon, riding high, foreshortened the restless shadows aboard the brig and drenched her with colorless light. The ringing of the *Somers'* bell broke time into half-hour lengths, and the lookout, responding to the measured clangor, wailed that all was well. In the night's ever more silent advance, the rhythmic crashing at the vessel's bows was like a vast creature's breathing.

The bell struck eight times. The *Somers* had dropped another day behind her. It had been, the logbook entries indicated, fair, mild, uneventful. The brig was to know no such serenity in the days immediately ahead.

One slight event of this lately departed Friday may have had melancholy significance. Acting Midshipman John Tillotson, this Friday evening, saw the Negro wardroom steward, Waltham, bring half a tumbler of liquor into the steerage and hand it to Spencer, who put it in his locker. Later, he took it out again and gave it to Small.

This may have been the last of the favors that Elisha Small, at a final exorbitant price, obtained from his superior.

CHAPTER 6

Saturday, November 26

"This Greek document is the official record of the mutinous conspiracy, prepared by the chief conspirator and, like the other records, contains on its face . . . the stamp of incontestible verity."—ALEXANDER SLIDELL MACKENZIE.

THE SUN had risen hours before; the *Somers'* crew had begun the day's work, but James W. Wales, the lately quaking repository of plans for mutiny, still took his time. Long afterward, he was to write, as extenuation for his delay, that he was hampered all this Saturday by Small and Cromwell, who *"dogged"* him.

That, and other amendments he made to his original statement, may or may not have been true. We have only the fact that it was not till seven o'clock, or after, that Wales gave the alarm. Even at that late hour, he was a deliberate herald of calamity.

The purser's steward began at the bottom. He sidled into the wardroom and, finding Purser Heiskill there, told him what had happened the night before. Wales, afflicted by extreme modesty, then went back on deck, found Gansevoort, and reported that Mr. Heiskill would like to see the lieutenant in the wardroom.

Thus, the dreadful tidings went upward through channels, tardily and deliberately. Gansevoort, alarmed, scuttled to the cabin and blurted the tale to Mackenzie, who laughed at him.

"*Ridiculous!*" he scoffed.

He laughed again, probably for the last time in the five days of waxing torment that now were beginning.

"*It's impossible,*" the commander pursued, a shade more gravely. "*Someone has been spinning a wild yarn. It couldn't be. The vessel is in a good state of discipline.*"

"*Yes, sir.*"

"A *good state of discipline,*" the commander repeated. "*You know that yourself, Mr. Gansevoort.*"

"*Yes, sir.*"

The captain of the *Somers* stared thoughtfully for a moment at the calm blue sky beyond the cabin skylight. He heard the morning's routine progressing normally on the deck above him.

"*Not a vestige of truth in it,*" he said loudly. "*Mr. Spencer is addicted to romances and has been amusing himself at Wales's expense.*"

"*Yes, sir.*"

"*Nevertheless,*" Mackenzie pursued, twisting about in his chair, "*this is joking upon an improper theme.*"

The instant when panic begins seldom has been so precisely fixed. The commander's late skepticism was wavering and in that hesitant moment the obscure and dreadful thing —terror, hysteria, or undetermined mental pestilence—came aboard the brig to flitter into hiding and incubate there.

Gansevoort, his superior's mirror, saluted and turned away. Mackenzie's eyes were troubled.

"*Stay,*" he bade, and his face puckered with thought. "*It may possibly—just possibly—be that there is a—well, a grain of truth in all this bilge. Mr. Spencer is a—reckless young man. It might be well, Mr. Gansevoort, if he were kept under close observation for a time. You, sir, will be pleased to follow him.*"

Watch him carefully, but on no account let him be aware of it. And send Wales to me."

"Aye aye, sir."

The personified echo of Alexander Slidell Mackenzie's every belief and judgment saluted again and went away. His superior, having thrust the problem into Gansevoort's hands, found himself unable to leave it there. While he waited for Wales, the commander marshaled excuses for his own uneasiness.

Acting Midshipman Spencer was the black sheep of Mackenzie's flock: a base person, a drinker, a brand destined for the burning. He fraternized with the crew, stayed aloof from the company of officers and gentlemen, and even had dared to jeer at his captain.

Not to Mackenzie's face, of course. In contacts with him, Mr. Spencer had been excessively, almost derisively, polite, yet there was something about him, something leering in his eye, that was furtively villainous.

The commander sighed. If he had been able to transfer this troublesome young man before the *Somers* had sailed, apprehensions—doubtless unjustified—would not be filling the cabin now.

There was one plausibility, at least, Mackenzie mused, in the wild yarn. Spencer, indeed, was intimate with Small. Could they, together, truly be plotting mutiny? The acting midshipman was even more friendly with Cromwell. Was he among the twenty desperadoes who were said to be preparing to take the brig? Cromwell would be a formidable mutineer. Where was Wales? Why didn't he report?

The purser's steward, finally appearing, recited at length to a troubled listener the tale of his interview with Spencer.

The lately discredited young man could not have overlooked this opportunity to reburnish his own reputation and further blacken Spencer's. He must have submitted for his captain's enlightenment samples, at least, from the carefully assembled collection of the acting midshipman's misdeeds, for by the time the conference ended, Mackenzie was badly shaken.

Wales emerged from the cabin with the feeling that he had done very well for himself. He had impressed the commander with his own assiduity and loyalty. He thought he had erased from his superior's plainly agitated mind any lingering resentment concerning that unfortunate deal in Puerto Rico.

Alone and sweltering in his cabin, the captain of the *Somers* tried with small success to resist the beliefs that pressed in upon him. None of the salutary amusement roused by Gansevoort's tidings came to Mackenzie's rescue now. The tale, as Wales had told it, made a once preposterous yarn seem possible, almost probable.

Suppose the brig actually were captured by mutinous scoundrels and turned into a pirate craft! Mackenzie knew what ghastliness she might wreak. He was familiar with the atrocities perpetrated by pirates. He had learned much of their savagery while attached, long ago, to the squadron that had sailed to suppress these monsters.

And the *Somers*, herself, would make a terrible sea raider. The utmost malevolence could not have designed her more perfectly for a black career. There was more than coincidence here. Evil forces, bent on destruction, were all about the commander. Fright carried him further:

"An American vessel of war was about to become a pirate cruiser. A vessel which had been born into our national family and consecrated as a defender of our country's glory and one of the great protectors of the commonwealth of civilized man [sic] *was about to be torn free from her sphere and let loose, a lawless wanderer upon the deep, carrying along in her devi-*

ous course, like a comet loosed from its orbit, devastation and terror and death. Perhaps no vessel could be found, better fitted to become the pest of the ocean."

So Mackenzie wrote, looking back months later on this day of dreadful revelation. Before Saturday had ended, he had worked himself into a dangerously excited state. The jumble of inconsequences, irrelevances, and intuitions that Guert Gansevoort brought back from his sleuthing had done nothing to soothe his superior.

The lieutenant had had an emotionally and physically depleting day. He possessed little of the fortitude or resourcefulness successful detection demands, and he lacked almost entirely the ability to evaluate his findings. Mr. Gansevoort stole about the brig with an ill-fitting air of unconcern and tried with indifferent success to keep Spencer under continual observation without arousing his suspicions.

Through a crack in the wardroom door, the lieutenant had watched his quarry for some time. The boy had been sitting *"rather sullenly in a corner of the steerage as was his custom."* Spencer had written on a paper with a pencil and had whittled away at the tail bone of a devilfish that he was carving into a ring for his cravat.

Later, sleuth Gansevoort had been lurking within earshot while the suspect had pored over charts of the West Indies. Dr. Leecock had been present, and Spencer had asked him whether he were familiar with the Isle of Pines. The brig's surgeon had chuckled.

"A notorious haunt for pirates," he had replied. *"Have you friends there?"* and Spencer had grinned.

The lieutenant had tiptoed away, dizzied by the importance of his find. It was the sole valid bit of evidence, though no more than corroborative, that his prying and shadowing were to produce.

Gansevoort, while attempting to remain inconspicuous, went round and round and up and down. He stole about the deck behind Spencer. He climbed after the boy into the foretop, and there surprised him in the act of getting himself tattooed by Benjamin F. Green, first-class apprentice. Green was inking the suspect's forearm, not with a skull and crossbones, but with "a love device."

The lieutenant, as the day advanced, swept further rubbish into his bag. Spencer had inspected the chronometer and had asked Midshipman Henry Rogers about its rate. He had read Rogers' palm and predicted his early death.

Detective work unsettled the detective's sensibilities, making them peculiarly vulnerable to the shock they sustained late that afternoon. Gansevoort identified the incident as revelation and, practically, confession.

The weary and somewhat footsore shadow had followed Spencer to the foot of the foremast. The boy started to climb up the Jacob's ladder. Then he turned and looked down at the aghast Gansevoort.

"He kept staring at me with the most infernal expression I have ever beheld on a human face. It satisfied me of his guilt."

That look may have expressed diabolical iniquity. It may equally well have been due to nothing more sinister than a natural exasperation toward the man who had been treading on Spencer's heels all day long.

Gansevoort's mind, stampeded by an *"infernal expression,"* still was running away with him when, shortly before evening quarters, he presented his findings to Mackenzie. Apprehension had magnified the suspect's glare and his questions concerning a map and a clock into tacit admissions of guilt. Then, as thereafter, the oversized fears of commander and lieutenant hustled them onward.

"And what, sir," Mackenzie demanded, when Gansevoort had completed his dire report, "would you do with Mr. Spencer if you were in my situation?"

"Arrest him, sir," Gansevoort prescribed valiantly. "Arrest him, iron him, and keep him on the quarter-deck."

"My intention precisely, Mr. Gansevoort. I am glad you agree with me."

The prologue ends here, and the tragedy proper begins. It was not to be primarily a struggle between lawful authority and rebellion. That motive was secondary, scarcely more than incidental.

The Somers mutiny, in essence, was a losing conflict between hitherto respectable men and compelling fear that, first and mysteriously, beset their commander and, swiftly spreading, infected all his officers, save one, whom they slew.

No one can tell whence the terror came or why it grew so great. Records more than a century old detail the frightful consequences. They do not explain the nature of the frenzy; they do not specifically admit that it existed.

At the tragedy's opening, and continually thereafter, the tormented mind of Alexander Slidell Mackenzie seized every opportunity for ceremony as though this might hide extremity. It is not clear whether, to grace the tragedy's first scene, he followed his usual bent and put on his dress uniform. Certainly, he ornately arrayed his spirit.

The drummer beat, the fifer shrilled the call to evening quarters. Feet thudded along the deck as the crew took their stations. Mackenzie, emerging from his cabin, reset the stage.

All officers, save for the midshipman forward, were ordered to gather around their captain. Sailing Master Perry took the wheel, and enlisted men were banished from the quarter-deck.

When all had been arranged to his liking, the commander turned to Spencer and spoke the first line of the part he had prepared for himself:

"*I learn, Mr. Spencer, that you aspire to the command of the* Somers."

The bolt missed fire. The boy whom Mackenzie had expected to wither only smiled at him and shook his head.

"*Oh, no, sir.*"

The commander let go a verbal broadside.

"*Did you not tell Mr. Wales, sir, that you had a plan to kill the commander, the officers, and a considerable portion of the crew of this vessel and convert her into a pirate?*"

This blast, too, flew wide. Spencer replied quite easily:

"*I may have told him so, sir, but in joke.*"

The boy was taking insolent liberties with the script Mackenzie had prepared. He had not blanched or cringed. Under the gaping scrutiny of the hitherto unapprised officers and the more remote stares of the crew, Spencer was maintaining a self-possession that properly belonged to his accuser, who now cried out:

"*This, sir, is joking on a forbidden subject. This 'joke' may cost you your life. Be pleased to remove your neck handkerchief.*"

Spencer obeyed. The kerchief was empty, and when Mackenzie, thwarted again, demanded the paper that had been hidden there, he was told, still calmly:

"*It was a paper containing my day's work, and I have destroyed it.*"

"*It was a singular place to keep your day's work.*"

"It was a convenient one," the acting midshipman replied with what his inquisitor considered a maddening *"air of deference and blandness."*

Mackenzie frantically tried to get back the scene his opponent was stealing. Inflating, the captain of the *Somers* delivered his big speech:

"You must have been aware that you could only have compassed your designs by passing over my dead body and, after that, the bodies of all the officers. You have given yourself, sir, a great deal to do. It will be necessary for me to confine you, sir."

Mackenzie wheeled and raised his voice even higher.

"Mr. Gansevoort, arrest Mr. Spencer and put him in double irons."

A windy sound, not uttered by the breeze, ran along the deck as the brig's second-in-command stepped forward and detached the prisoner's sword. Gansevoort hesitated, then asked:

"Have you weapons concealed on your person?"

"No," Spencer answered, then added with bitterness: *"You had better overhaul me, though. No one will believe anything I say, now."*

The lieutenant's search revealed nothing more incriminating than *"some scraps of paper and part of an old pipe."* He turned and beckoned to Garty, the laden master-at-arms.

Double irons were clamped on the boy's ankles; heavy handcuffs were snapped over his wrists. The weight of all this hardware made it difficult to stand up and impossible to walk unaided. Spencer was helped, lurching and clanking, to the larboard arms chest, far aft on the quarter-deck, seated there, and committed by the commander to Gansevoort's care.

"Put him to death at once, sir," Mackenzie ordered, *"if he*

tries to hold communication with any member of the crew. At the same time," he added, somewhat confusingly, *"accord him every comfort that his safekeeping will admit of."*

These singular instructions were obeyed by the lieutenant in an unusual fashion that the captain of the *Somers* found more than satisfactory.

"Throughout the period of Mr. Spencer's confinement," Mackenzie assured the Secretary of the Navy, *"Mr. Gansevoort, while watching over his person with an eagle eye and ready at any moment to take his life . . . ministered in every way to his comfort with the tenderness of a woman."*

The conspiracy had been beheaded, its designer, captured; yet Mackenzie's and Gansevoort's minds were still troubled. There had been an ominous quality to Spencer's calm submission. Perhaps that strange self-possession was due to the belief that he shortly would be rescued by fellow mutineers. His arrest might not have averted revolt. Instead, it might have expedited it!

As for the crew, Mackenzie and Gansevoort did not like their behavior, either. They were agitated; they kept staring aft. They gathered in groups and talked. Thenceforth, the *Somers'* officers were to read dire portents into everything the crew did.

The brig picked up her evening routine again. Batteries were inspected, reports received, and at last retreat was beaten. Mackenzie, still disturbed, departed from usage at this point.

Except for men on duty there, all members of the crew were to stay off the quarter-deck and, furthermore, keep well forward. That would increase the safety of the brig during the night that was already falling.

Joseph Sears, second-class apprentice, while moving obediently forward, fell in with Elisha Small and asked him what all the fuss had been about.

There had been some foolish talk about mutiny, Small told the boy, but nothing would come of it. It was Small's opinion that Mr. Spencer was *"half crazy, half out of his head."*

Far wilder theories have been advanced to explain the *Somers* affair.

The little seaman was taken ill that night. Worry may have sickened him. Spencer had been ironed for mutiny, and Small had been his eager beneficiary, who had tolerated the boy's wild talk for the gifts of cash, tobacco, and liquor that had accompanied it. The boy was in bad trouble now and, conceivably, his crony might be, too.

Small's misery would have been increased had he known that searchers of Spencer's locker already had discovered, in an otherwise empty razor case, three sheets of paper.

One, enclosed within the others, bore three names: George A. Brest, Frederick Wells, and Edward Roberts. There were no such persons aboard the brig, and this paper's significance was never established. The remaining two pages, old, creased, and soiled, were Philip Spencer's fanciful or actual outline for mutiny.

The larger sheet, of ordinary writing paper, bore columns of characters, entirely unfamiliar to their finders. The accompanying page had been torn from a geometry textbook. One side bore the printed diagram of a theorem; the other was covered with writing in the same blind script. Here was possible evidence, but the searchers were unable to read it until Midshipman Rogers, the brig's man of erudition, discovered that Spencer had used the Greek alphabet to set down English words. Henceforth, the two sheets were called "the Greek Paper."

The larger exhibit was a roster and, with corrections of Spencer's misspelling, read in translation:

Certain	*To Be Kept, Nolens Volens*
P. Spencer	Sibley
E. Andrews	Stremel
D. McKinley	Scott
Wales	Van Brunt
	Smith
Doubtful	Whitmore
Wilson X	Gagely
McKee X	Blackwell
Warner	Rodman
Green	Clark
Van Velsor	Knevels
Sullivan	Keily
Godfrey	Velsor
Callia X	Corney
Howard X	Dickenson
	The Doctor
	Garrebrantz
	Waltham

The writing on the smaller page apparently was intended to be a watch bill—a schedule of the posts the conspirators were to take at the moment of mutiny. It read:

Wheel	McKee
Arms Chest	McKinley

	Spencer
Cabin	Small
	Wilson
Wardroom	Spencer
	Spencer
Steerage	Small
	Wilson

Below this list and still in Greek script was written:

Those marked X will probably be induced to join before the project is carried into execution. The remainder of the doubtful will probably join when the thing is done; if not, they must be forced. If any not marked down wish to join after it is done, we will pick out the best and dispose of the rest.

Probabilities have been pulled to pieces by appraisers of this singular document. Mackenzie professed to consider it absolute proof that mutiny, completely planned and full-statured, was about to explode. Defenders of Philip Spencer's memory, in 1842 and later, drew from the Greek Paper conclusions no more fantastic.

The roster and watch bill, some persons have contended, had been compiled as an idle amusement by a lonely and maladjusted boy. Others, ignoring inconvenient facts, have maintained that the paper was only a list of men Spencer hoped to engage for a trading voyage to the Pacific coast. Members of the fraternity the youngster had helped to found have advanced the theory that their Chi Psi brother was engaged in nothing more sinister than the formation of a seagoing Greek-letter society.

It is doubtful how serious were Spencer's rebellious intentions. It is still more questionable whether a single shipmate genuinely shared them, yet the scribblings, however vague and contradictory, must have been an outline for mutiny. As such, they were as ill-prepared and poorly presented as their author's college recitations.

There is, at the outset, the question of the number of Spencer's accomplices. He boasted to Wales that there were twenty. The list cited as "certain" only four, including the purser's steward, and leaving, without him, only three. Since Wales maintained that he never actually enlisted in the plot, it is permissible to wonder whether Spencer's remaining fellow mutineers were more firmly committed.

It is true that ten men and boys, including my great-uncle, were set down as *"doubtful,"* but only four of these, the paper indicated, would *"probably be induced to join before the project is carried into execution."* Thus the twenty determined rebels shrink under inspection to a dubious seven, including the plotter-in-chief. Six mutineers would have been an unimpressive force to lead against a hundred-odd members of the *Somers'* company. Nevertheless, Spencer had told Garty that six men could take the brig.

There is also the problem of "E. Andrews" who was listed as one of the four *"certain"* mutineers. Mackenzie maintained on purely inspirational warrant that "Andrews" was an alias for Cromwell. Spencer told Gansevoort that "Andrews" was Small's real name. It was all most confusing to increasingly frightened minds.

Besides, if "Andrews" stood for Cromwell in the roster of already enlisted conspirators, why was Small's name not there, too? He is cited twice in the watch bill for revolt. Cromwell's name does not appear on this, either.

The Greek Paper is contradictory and cryptic today largely

because the captain of the *Somers* and his officers made no intelligent and purposeful attempt to persuade the author to explain the puzzle. Gansevoort, in one of his more valiant moments, did try to trap Spencer into self-condemnation, but the lieutenant's questions were few and halfhearted and got him nowhere.

It was panic's dilating influence that made the more than ordinarily slipshod work of a not very bright youngster appear dreadfully evidential. Spencer's plan, whether earnestly intended or not, was ridiculous on the face of it. He gave leading roles in his conspiracy to persons not listed as "certain" mutineers. He blundered, stumbled, and confounded himself.

Spencer, by the Greek Paper's testimony, was to undertake to deal with the wardroom's occupants. He informed Wales that he intended to slaughter them all. Yet one of those occupants—Dr. Leecock—is listed as among the persons the conspiracy's inventor intended to keep, willy-nilly.

Philip Spencer made a characteristic botch of his outline for mutiny, yet, for men already possessed, the smudged, scrawled pages with their flagrant errors and comic spelling tightened the grip of terror.

There are other errors and discrepancies, not of Spencer's making, to be cited at the close of this, the first day of the agonized five. Mackenzie, when warned by Gansevoort of impending mutiny, scoffed at the tidings and insisted that the brig was "in a good state of discipline." Much later, he was to maintain in his report that discipline had begun to deteriorate by the time the *Somers* had sailed from Madeira and that it had continued to fall apart until after the hangings. The statements collide head on. Furthermore, after the conference with Wales, the commander ignored his obvious duty and turned his back upon elemental common sense.

Spencer, on the night of November 25, had promised to tell
Wales more about the projected mutiny the next day. Mackenzie did not order the purser's steward to seek out the mutineer-
in-chief and question him. Mackenzie did not summon Spencer and interrogate the boy himself; nor did he examine Small;
nor did he ever bring accused and accuser before him and
conduct even an informal inquiry.

The captain of the *Somers*, supreme aboard her, quite easily
could have obtained solutions to questions now unanswerable,
yet he made not the least effort to acquire them; he shrank
from the idea. To the commander's apprehensive mind, veri-
ties became too terrible to face; they were horrid facts of life,
never to be bared or mentioned openly. His imitative officers
preserved a like modesty. The frenzy that overtook the brig
was highly contagious.

No one can tell how accurately James W. Wales, facile
editor and expander of his own written statement, reported
his dark conference with Spencer. It seems reasonably certain
that the purser's steward, during his tattling to Mackenzie,
implicated Cromwell in the plot, on no better warrant than
that the acting boatswain was the chief plotter's friend.

Spencer did not say that Cromwell was in the conspiracy.
Spencer, indeed, during the brief remainder of his life, repeatedly absolved his crony from any complicity. But Cromwell
had scoffed at the confusion aboard the brig when Mackenzie
had beat to quarters; Cromwell had God-damned the Mackenzie jib lacing. Wales just guessed that the bellowing acting
boatswain was a mutineer. The presumption was not unpleasant to the commander.

In the mental and moral chaos about to be loosed aboard

the *Somers,* a guess could be as damning as a confession of guilt.

There was further misapprehension and negligence. Apart from Spencer's "infernal" expression, the items in detective Gansevoort's haul that he had considered most incriminating were the suspect's inquiry about the rate of the chronometer and his prediction that Midshipman Rogers would meet an untimely end.

Spencer and Rogers had bet on the time of the brig's arrival at St. Thomas. Without knowledge of the chronometer's rate, the acting midshipman could not have plotted the *Somers'* position. Furthermore, he had predicted, in obvious jest, that Rogers would die a gambler's death. The wager, incidentally, involved a bottle of brandy.

These absolving facts were not discovered until later. Inquiry would have established them at once, but Mackenzie and his subordinates didn't like to ask questions.

Officers on duty, that night of November 26, were ordered by Mackenzie to carry sword and pistol and to patrol the brig continually. They stole about, flinching at sudden sounds, shying away from dark nooks and corners. Lieutenant Gansevoort stood beside the manacled boy on the arms chest, ready to slaughter him or minister to his wants with feminine tenderness, as the occasion required.

The *Somers'* bell was rung eight times, and the day ended. In its duration, no mutinous act had been attempted, no mutinous word spoken.

CHAPTER 7

Sunday, November 27

*"The fire beneath the surface which causes the earthquake
reserves for the hour of the explosion its more palpable and
awful demonstrations."*—ALEXANDER SLIDELL MACKENZIE.

DESPITE THE nightlong apprehensions of the armed
patrols, the sudden tropical dawn found little changed aboard
the *Somers*, this fateful Sabbath. A following wind blew
freshly, waves blithely unfurled their banners of foam, and the
long, young sunlight was turning the sails to gold.

Presently, the brig's deck resounded to the thump of holy-
stones and the plash of water. A chained and desolate figure,
sitting beside the larboard arms chest, was the only strangeness
apparent on this otherwise normal morning, but the minds of
Philip Spencer's captors were greatly disturbed.

The empty game of "pussy wants a corner" they had played
throughout the night with invisible mutineers had further unsettled the *Somers'* officers. None of them was as thoroughly
upset as their captain, although the fearful Lieutenant Gansevoort again was searching, this time on his own responsibility,
for further evidence of impending revolt.

Mackenzie informed Mr. Upshur that, during the dark
hours, some member of the crew had talked with Philip Spencer. The commander's report doesn't tell how he found out
or how, with the prisoner continually under the eagle eye of

Gansevoort and armed officers prowling about, such a conference had been possible.

Fife and drum called the crew to morning quarters and inspection at ten o'clock. The commander, brilliant in full uniform but inwardly bedeviled, took station where he could watch Small and Cromwell closely. Both suspects were members of the master's division, which mustered along the quarterdeck, extending the parallel lines of men and boys in dress whites who stood, facing inward, behind the guns.

Cromwell and Small were faultlessly uniformed. Mackenzie's mind at once leaped to the clairvoyant conclusion that here was an indication that both men had something to hide. He thought that Cromwell's appearance was *"determined and dangerous"* and found Small's *"ghastly."*

"He shifted his weight from side to side and his battle-axe passed from one hand to the other. His eye wandered irresolutely but never toward mine. I atttributed his conduct to fear."

The little man's shaken aspect might as well have been due to his illness of the night before and the physicking Dr. Leecock recently had administered, but the commander seldom inquired into causes.

When inspection had been completed and the brig's company had been mustered for church, Mackenzie sought further for a sign of impending mutiny. Beyond the fact that the crew seemed uncommonly attentive and their responses in the ritual unusually loud, the commander could discover no omen, yet the devout behavior of men and boys did nothing to allay his fears. These were increased, soon after services had ended.

Gansevoort, the inspirational inspector of countenances, had found another face that had frightened him. The acting boatswain's grim expression, his apparent refusal to meet his superior's eye, alarmed the lieutenant, who confided:

"*I don't like Cromwell's looks.*"

No further irregularity, intuitional or actual, disturbed the brig for the rest of the morning. Her company's conduct was normal, save for the plight of Philip Spencer, hunched down by the arms chest and still unquestioned. It was not until afternoon that Mackenzie found further reason for alarm.

The wind slackened after midday, and the captain of the *Somers* ordered that her royal topgallant and skysails be set. The slender, rakishly slanting mainmast of the brig was rigged to carry five successive tiers of canvas majestically in light airs: mainsail, topsail, topgallant sail, royal topgallant sail, and uppermost and precariously borne on the slenderest segment of the mast, the skysail.

Mackenzie's order had just been executed, and Ward M. Gagely, first-class apprentice, was still balanced far aloft on the mainmast's royal yardarm when a sharp crack roused shouting on the deck and in the rigging.

The topgallant mast had snapped. Carrying the recently set sails along, it buckled, to dangle upside down, a flapping welter of wood, canvas, and rigging. Gagely kept his head and his footing and was unhurt, though he might easily enough have been cast down to the deck or into the sea.

The orders he was obliged to bellow through less purposeful outcry kept Mackenzie, for the moment, from reading any dark significance into an accident of frequent occurrence on square-riggers. While he watched seamen swarm up to the site of the mishap, he "*did not dream that the carrying away of the mast was an act of treachery.*"

But, when the excitement had boiled away and repairs had begun, the commander had time to think. Habitually, he thought too much, and by now his mind had been leashed to the dread word "mutiny." He might move away to the limit of his tether, but he could not escape.

Might not this apparent accident have been contrived by Philip Spencer's accomplices, who were still at large; might they not have intended to knock young Gagely off the yardarm and, in the consequent confusion, revolt, rescue the mutineer-in-chief, and take the brig?

The waking nightmare Mackenzie was creating acquired additional substance when he learned that Elisha Small had been at least partly responsible for the mishap. He had hauled on the weather main-royal brace, the commander reported to the Secretary of the Navy, with another miscreant, "*whose name I have not discovered,*" and the tip of the mainmast had carried away.

And that was not all, Mackenzie assured Mr. Upshur. To the astonishment and horror of the captain of the *Somers,* "*all those who were most conspicuously named in the program of Mr. Spencer, no matter in what part of the ship they might be stationed, mustered at the main-topmast head.*"

"*Whether,*" the commander wrote archly, "*animated by some newborn zeal in the service of their country or collected there for the purpose of conspiring, it was not easy to decide. The coincidence confirmed the existence of a dangerous conspiracy, suspended yet perhaps not abandoned.*"

While the men aloft, conspirators or not, were clearing away and lowering the wreckage, Mackenzie's apprehensive eyes lit upon a fresh incitement to fright. He decided, with intuition worthy of Gansevoort, that Philip Spencer, crouching on the quarter-deck beneath the weight of his chains, was attempting to communicate at long range with accomplices at the topmast head. The prisoner *"cast thither many of the strange and stealthy glances I had heretofore noticed."*

For which the archmutineer could have been pardoned. Weighted into helplessness by his irons as he was, the persistence of his upward glances might have been due to nothing more conspiratorial than a purely personal concern, lest the mess of wreckage tear loose and fall upon him.

Sergeant Garty, an only slightly less fluent informer than James W. Wales, bore to the commander this afternoon tidings that not only complicated his mental condition but also principally qualified Great-uncle George for the chains later bestowed on him.

Young Warner, Garty muttered, had commented unfavorably, while lashing his hammock that morning, on the fact that all of the *Somers'* officers were stalking about, heavily armed.

"I said they were and that I thought it was no more than was necessary. He said: 'What could they do if we made a rush at them in mid-watch?' I told him that if they did, thirteen or fourteen of them would drop. It ended there."

To overstrained minds, Garty's tale was the decisive factor in a day already heavy with evil portents. Small's reported responsibility for the breakage of the mast, his aspect at muster, Cromwell's aspect, Spencer's aspect, the plotters at the masthead, the mysterious conference on the previous night between the prisoner and an unidentified accomplice, and now George Warner's indiscretion, produced, by Mackenzie's peculiar method of addition, a horrifying total.

The day was almost spent. The *Somers* was brandishing her bowsprit at the low, red sun. Wicked men were still loose aboard the brig—conspiring men, mutinous men—and of these Acting Boatswain Samuel Cromwell was the greatest in stature and therefore, in Mackenzie's judgment, the greatest menace.

Night would be unbearably dreadful if Cromwell were still at large. The commander, on no better warrant, determined to arrest the man. He was still aloft, directing repairs. There would be time to submit the project to Mr. Gansevoort.

The lieutenant agreed. Strangely enough, he had been thinking the very same thing. The acting boatswain should be ironed, but he was a large man, a violent man. He might resist and set off the mutinous explosion.

Perhaps it would be better if all the officers collaborated in his arrest. Mackenzie was unarmed, and Gansevoort had only his sword and a newfangled Colt "repeating pistol."

Supper was piped. Mackenzie and his officers assembled at the foot of the mainmast. When Cromwell slid down to the deck, they closed in about him and immediately were all in deadly peril. A flash and a sharp report blasted the formalities of arrest. Gansevoort gaped sheepishly at the smoking revolver in his hand. In his nervousness he had discharged it but, fortunately, into the deck.

Mackenzie picked up his violently interrupted announcement and finished arresting Cromwell. The man submitted meekly enough. He was marched to the quarter-deck and made to sit down while he, like Spencer, was double-ironed. Thereafter, Mackenzie questioned him concerning the secret conference someone had had with the acting midshipman on Saturday night.

"*Sir,*" Cromwell said earnestly, "*it wasn't me; sir, it must have been Small.*"

Small thereupon was arrested by a smaller task force and with no inadvertent pistol shots. He was ironed and then half-carried to a place not far from Spencer and near the aftermost larboard carronade. Cromwell was deposited beside the starboard arms chest, across the quarter-deck from the acting midshipman.

Oliver Browning, boatswain's mate, was promoted into Cromwell's place by Mackenzie and William Collins, gunner's mate, into Browning's.

The brief twilight was thickening. The men and boys, off watch, had gone below to supper. What should have been a tranquil and restorative time for Mr. Gansevoort, who recently had barely missed shooting himself or someone else, was disturbed by further incident. A seaman reported that Mr. Spencer earnestly wished to speak to the lieutenant.

The prisoner, when Gansevoort joined him, wasted no words. He nodded toward the manacled giant on the quarter-deck's far side. Had Cromwell been arrested because of his intimacy with Philip Spencer? The lieutenant admitted warily that that could have been the reason. The prisoner's irons clanked as he earnestly leaned forward.

"Cromwell," Spencer insisted in a tight voice, "is innocent. That is the truth, Mr. Gansevoort."

The boy hesitated. Then he shrugged and said with a trace of bitterness:

"I doubt if Cromwell ever could have been enlisted in any such enterprise, unless there was money aboard."

Gansevoort did not ask Spencer to explain that slightly cryptic judgment. The lieutenant, rallying from momentary belief that the boy had spoken truthfully, told himself that Spencer for some dark purpose was extremely anxious to have Cromwell released.

No further questions were asked by prisoner or captor. After momentary silence, Gansevoort tiptoed away, closing a conversation that might have been enlightening if the lieutenant had been more persistent.

Spencer had been willing to talk. If Gansevoort had been adroit, he might have got from the prisoner admissions that would have placed in loyal hands priceless information concerning the scope and substance of the plot, granting that it had either.

But the lieutenant attempted no further inquiry. If his unconfirmed suspicions were so frightening, reality, plainly revealed, might be unbearably terrible.

Darkness closed in on the sea and the dim particle that was the stricken brig. Mackenzie and Gansevoort paced the quarter-deck together, keeping well away from the ironbound prisoners and talking in unconsciously hushed voices of what new peril the black hours ahead might spawn.

The wreckage at the mainmast's tip had been cleared before the men had been piped down to supper. A new spar had been broken out and lay along the deck, ready to be hoisted. It was deep night when those who had supped came up on deck again. The fitful wind uttered long-drawn, eerie sounds. Each small noise of the brig's passage plucked at Mackenzie's and Gansevoort's nerves. Beyond these petty disturbances lay a vast quiet, not tranquil but taut, as though the evening held its breath.

Then suddenly out of the gloom forward, it came. The dreadfulness that the officers had feared roused and surged toward them. With trampling of feet and gabbling outcry, a black mass moved aft. Gansevoort shrilled:

"God! I believe they're coming!"

He drew his revolver. Mackenzie gasped, whirled about, and

dived into his cabin to arm himself. The lieutenant leaped upon the trunk and ran forward along it toward the danger. He leveled his weapon.

"*Halt!*" Gansevoort yelled. "*Halt, I say! I'll blow out the brains of the first man who steps on the quarter-deck.*"

He checked the advance. The crowd babbled protests, not threats, and its foremost members shrank back from the wabbling pistol. From the rear of the press, Midshipman Rogers lifted a quavering voice:

"*Mr. Gansevoort! Don't shoot, sir. We're coming aft to man the mast rope; that's all.*"

And that *was* all, yet it was some time before the commander and his lieutenant could be convinced. Mackenzie, who had run below—to get a gun—when the men had advanced, and Gansevoort, who again had barely missed shooting someone by mistake, found it hard to believe that the crew had not been in revolt but had been obeying an order.

Dread already had stripped the minds of the *Somers'* captain, his lieutenant, and their subordinate officers so bare that the impress of new fright was difficult, and often impossible, to eradicate.

It had been Rogers' own empty apprehensions that had caused the terrifying movement aft. The men had stayed well forward when they had come up from supper. That was where Mackenzie had ordered them to remain, after dark, and remain there they would.

Collins, lately promoted to acting boatswain's mate and filled with new authority, had come among the loiterers and had ordered them aft to man the mast rope that would carry the new spar aloft. His audience had laughed at him. They weren't having any, not with three prisoners already ironed for undiscernible offenses, not while Mr. Gansevoort was aft with that self-discharging pistol. And who did Collins think he was, anyway?

The new acting boatswain's mate, smarting under their derision, reported it to Midshipman Rogers. His already smoldering suspicions sprang into a blaze. Derision! Disobedience! Good God! This might be the very beginning of mutiny; it must be stamped out.

Rogers drew his pistol, yelled for Browning, the newly made acting boatswain, to follow him, and stormed in among the lounging dissenters.

"Get aft, d'ye hear me? Obey orders; aft, smartly. Browning, use your colt."

Boys yelped as the lash stung them. Men tried to explain their reluctance to Rogers while his brandished pistol and the acting boatswain's hard-plied colt drove them. The confusion that Mackenzie and Gansevoort misidentified as an uprising was nothing more deadly than the effort of crew members to escape a flogging or a bullet.

The captain of the *Somers* and his lieutenant, when the brief tumult had ended and its causes had been explained, were temporarily reassured. Later, when the strange seizure that afflicted them had grown still more acute, they were to return again to this incident and give it chief place among the portents of mutiny they believed that this day had brought forth. They were to make of this *"rush aft"* an even more sinister happening than the carrying away of the skysail.

Mackenzie and his officers blew up to the bursting point every least incident that fevered minds could possibly transform into a mutinous intention. The *Somers,* until the frenzy was appeased by the sacrifice of three men, was either a floating bedlam with the most demented residents in charge or a craft that, for no clear cause, had been infected by a vast, distorting terror.

Officers of a United States man-of-war were driven to extremity by a conspiracy that consisted, on the evidence, of a man and a boy—the former a foolish alcoholic, the latter, a dunce. Elisha Small and Philip Spencer were the only suspects whose guilt was even half-proved. The contention that their alliance constituted a menace was almost as preposterous as the contenders' antic efforts to scotch it.

Calmly considered, none of the events of this lively Sabbath, which Mackenzie later described as a day of successive portents and perils, supplied any evidence of impending mutiny. The efficacy of the big lie had not been discovered in 1842, but the commander of the *Somers,* in his report to Mr. Upshur, did well enough with lesser mendacities and half-truths.

Mackenzie's flat statement that on Saturday night the manacled and closely guarded Spencer had a "secret conference" with some member of the crew exemplifies the commander's slight respect for facts. He does not say when this communion occurred or how it could possibly have taken place. He simply writes that it happened and lets the statement stand, unsupported, unexplained.

This is only one of the many parentless accusations the commander embodied in his report. He left these foundlings on the doorsteps of the men he had hanged, the further to discredit them and justify himself.

The sailor-author, furthermore, was not averse to setting down only half an incident if, by omission of the remainder, he could make it appear more damning. He wrote that Small's haul on the weather main-royal brace had carried away the skysail. Mackenzie forgot to add that he himself had ordered the haul and that his nephew, Oliver H. Perry, had passed the command on to Small. The commander reported that the little seaman had been aided by an accomplice *"whose name I have not discovered."* Everyone else on the brig appears to have known that Small's assistant was Henry Corney, second-class apprentice.

The incident of the broken mast is darkened by further misstatements. Mackenzie wrote that *"all those who were most conspicuously mentioned"* in the Greek Paper immediately mustered at the topmast head. He expected the Secretary of the Navy to believe that conspirators would go aloft and there, in the plainest possible view of the brig's entire company, catch up on their plotting.

And who gathered at the masthead? No person listed by Spencer as a *"certain"* mutineer, unless "E. Andrews" was an alias for Cromwell. He was there. It was a boatswain's duty to superintend repairs. Small was there, too, but he was captain of the maintop and should have been present. Of the men listed by Spencer as *"doubtful,"* only Wilson and Gedney were aloft. The rest of the repair party, Anderson and Golderman, had not been mentioned in the Greek Paper at all.

Injustices, spasmodic and only dimly motivated, were increasing aboard the brig this Sunday. They marked the advance of terror and were to grow in number and atrocity in the days ahead.

Cromwell was arrested, largely because Gansevoort did not like his looks, and Small was ironed on Cromwell's unsupported accusation. The lieutenant shied away from interrogation of the apparently willing Spencer.

Nevertheless, that Sabbath must have been less ominous in fact than Mackenzie and Gansevoort made it appear. Later they inflated both the mainmast accident and the rush aft of men and boys into attempts to take the brig.

The *Somers'* logbook contradicts them. An entry, made November 27, mentions the breakage of the mast and no more than mentions it. There is no allegation that it was carried away for a mutinous purpose. There is no mention whatever of that terrifying stampede aft.

Sunday ended with three prisoners on the quarter-deck, where that morning only one had been. The brig's officers had become still more alarmed, yet no mutinous word had been spoken this day; no demonstrably mutinous act had been attempted.

CHAPTER 8

Monday, November 28

"The slander, sometimes suggested, that the officers of the Somers were rendered nervous by unmanly fear betrays an ignorance of the case and of the true character of the American naval officers."—ALEXANDER SLIDELL MACKENZIE.

THIS DAY began briskly with a double flogging. All hands were piped to witness punishment, and Charles Lambert, apprentice, and Henry Waltham, wardroom steward, were beaten to the extent of the law. Lambert was charged with filching material used in weaving straw hats from the recently imperiled Gagely; Waltham, with stealing brandy for Philip Spencer.

Mackenzie termed these petty larcenies *"vile offenses"* and *"crimes of considerable magnitude."* He deemed the moment *"not a time to bring the discipline of the vessel to a stand"* and therefore prescribed the legal limit of twelve lashes.

The commander, when he had seen his men thrashed, was not entirely comforted. It seemed to him that his display of severity had fallen short of its purpose. Mackenzie still felt that he had not recovered complete control of his wind-driven little world, and the brightness of sun and sky and sea could not wholly dispel dark uncertainty from his spirit.

He had exercised his authority vigorously. Three chain-laden culprits lay on the quarter-deck, where yesterday there had been but one. Two more vile criminals had been sternly punished. No single flicker of resistance had been offered during the ironing of Spencer, Cromwell, and Small or the flogging of Lambert and Waltham. Nevertheless, Mackenzie believed mutiny—indefinable, invisible—still infected the crew.

Their behavior at the moment was satisfactory, yet who could tell what lurked behind the sober demeanor of seamen and apprentices or when *"the fire beneath the surface that causes the earthquake"* might erupt violently?

The captain of the *Somers* suppressed no single reflection of his own that his unselective mentality deemed worthy of permanence in print. No one can tell what thoughts—resigned, resentful, or childishly alarmed—wandered through the sullen mind of the captured and immobilized source of the waxing dread. No one at the time made any sustained effort to uncover them. Officers and crew, by Mackenzie's orders, left Philip Spencer severely alone.

For that reason, little is known of what went on behind the dark screen a maladjusted youngster held up between himself and the world. In the revealing, final hour, what was seen neither proves nor disproves his guilt. It only attests that, in extremity, a frightened boy rather piteously tried to comport himself like a man.

Spencer's shipmates thought that he bore himself as a prisoner with ease and confidence, because he had been told by Mackenzie, when arrested, that he would be taken back to New York for trial. However, that promise could not have been entirely reassuring. It meant, when the cruise had ended, that Philip would face once more a furiously aroused father.

For all his air of indifference, inwardly the boy must have quailed. He had done it again; it was all of one piece! He was still plodding the old, wretched circle. There never had been and there probably never would be anything else.

He had been kicked out of one college, jerked by an impatient paternal hand from another. He had been brought home in disgrace from his first cruise. He had been reinstated and now he was homeward-bound, in disgrace again. There was no end to it.

Once more he would endure, with inward quailing, the cutting words a thin and bitter mouth would fling at him, once more, suffer his mother's tears and reproaches. Once more, his father would threaten to disown him and then, when rage and invective had run out, would contrive some new, rehabilitating torment for his son. Trial and sentence, however severe, were easier to contemplate than the prospect of John Canfield Spencer's wrath.

It would be no ordinary anger, for this had been no ordinary offense. That, from the moment irons had been clapped on Philip, had become increasingly plain. This time, he had got not only himself but others into trouble. His two closest friends sat near him now, burdened like himself. He could find in their eyes when their glances crossed his, none of the respect and admiration that had pleased him so greatly and had moved him to many generosities. They looked at him a little as his father would when next he saw his son.

What Spencer had begun had not ended with the arrest of Cromwell and Small. The boy had started something that, by a strange momentum, still ran on. It was not a large vessel and, though he had been placed far aft, he was still in contact with her company. He could not tell what was happening, but he could see, hear, and feel the queer, frightening change. The way the officers watched him; the way the crew stared at him from a distance; the flurry of excitement last night when the commander had run below and the lieutenant had drawn his repeating pistol—all were part of it.

Though iron-burdened, helpless, and closely guarded, Philip Spencer must have felt that, in some dim fashion, he was responsible for the tension that enveloped the *Somers*.

If the principal prisoner was aware of a change in the atmosphere of the brig, her captain was excruciatingly conscious of it. The awful sounds of the previous night's stampede still echoed in his ears. Dread of another sinister accident like yesterday's on the mainmast bore down his heart.

Fear was pulling Mackenzie's fragile fortitude apart. He no longer was determined to rout out and punish the unarrested guilty. By his own words, he was willing to have them go away, hide themselves, leave him alone. He looked about him, fearful of further signs and portents.

The beaten apprentice was sniveling and caressing his ribs. The Negro, Waltham, was untied; his irons were clapped on him again, and he was hauled below. While in duress, the night before, he had told Daniel McKinley, one of the four men listed in the Creek Paper as committed mutineers, where three more bottles of brandy were hidden. McKinley, apparently to keep his own nose clean, had informed on the steward. Waltham was due for twelve more lashes on the morrow.

The fact that McKinley, a leading suspect, had joined the forces of law and order did not encourage Mackenzie. The fear that was to rule him increasingly in the days to come and blind him to facts, deafen him to probabilities, was already providing him with farfetched theories. He found McKinley's ratting *"an extraordinary denunciation under the circumstances, probably occasioned by his desire to relieve himself from suspicion."*

Something more should be done, the commander felt sure, to pacify the crew. He would address it personally. He did not dismiss the muster but climbed upon the trunk and cleared his throat. It had been several days since he had publicly exhorted his command. He must not be so laggard hereafter.

Mackenzie thereupon endeavored to exorcise mutiny by oratory—not forthrightly but with deviousness and delicacy. His crew was massed about him, but Spencer and his fellow prisoners were within easy earshot. The commander informed Secretary Upshur:

"I commenced by explaining to them the general nature of the project of Mr. Spencer, studiously avoiding to excite any suspicions that I was in the possession of the names of those who were implicated. I was willing, in fact, that the worst of them should repent and hide themselves among the well-disposed members of the crew."

This was not a schoolmistress discussing lewdness among the young ladies in the dormitory with a spinster's quailing reticence; this was the captain of a man-of-war, professedly faced with mutiny. It was also Alexander Slidell Mackenzie's report of his own speech.

"I endeavored to divert the minds of the slightly disaffected from the picture of successful vice which Mr. Spencer had presented to them. I alluded to the circumstances that the most of the crew [were?] unlike crews in general, having ties of kindred to render life dear to them and expressed the hope that within three weeks we should be again among our friends. I thanked God that we had friends to follow us with solicitude and affection; for to have friends and not to be unworthy of them was the best guarantee that could be given for truth and fidelity."

Mackenzie may not have deliberately pitched his voice so

that it would carry to his chief prisoner's ears. Certainly the boy could not have failed to hear most of the orator's dilation upon the evil that had been wrought by a monster of iniquity. It was voiced in a disconcertingly chilling fashion, as though Philip Spencer were not alive and listening, but already dead. Cromwell and Small were watching him. The boy pretended to ignore them.

When he had run out of eloquence, the commander hopefully surveyed his audience.

"*The effect upon them*" he confessed, "*was various. It filled many of them with horror at the idea of what they had escaped from. It inspired others with terror at dangers awaiting them from their connexion with the conspiracy. The thought of returning to that home and those friends from whom it had been intended to cut them off forever caused many of them to weep.*

"*I now,*" the commander reported with modest pride, "*considered the crew tranquillized and the vessel safe.*"

Whatever lapses are otherwise discernible in Commander Mackenzie's selective memory, it retained intact the details of his every public address.

In this instance, the speaker's satisfaction was short-lived. The same presumption that permitted him to diagram his hearers' emotions induced him to believe, with the glow of his performance still upon him, that Spencer was attempting "*to hold intelligence*" with the crew. Again, the commander does not say what these attempts were or how a closely guarded captive was able to make them.

To end such nefarious, if unspecified, endeavors, Mackenzie ordered Gansevoort to have the chain-burdened trio turned about so they would face aft. In that position, they could view only the brig's stern and, beyond it, the wind-blown curve of her wake, streaming away toward the unsteady horizon. Spencer, thus situated, must have felt still more desolately alone in a hostile world.

In waspish reprisal for the new fright the boy had caused him, the commander also told the lieutenant to take their tobacco from all three captives.

"Captain," Gansevoort said, returning, *"the prisoners are exceedingly distressed. They earnestly beg you to allow them tobacco."*

"Oh, no, Mr. Gansevoort," Mackenzie replied. *"Oh, no, indeed. You may go back and inform them that everything will be supplied them that is necessary for their health and comfort —but not tobacco.*

"Tobacco," he added primly, *"is a stimulant. Tell the prisoners I wish them to tranquillize their minds and remain free from excitement."*

All three men were habitual smokers. Spencer was particularly unmanned by this deprivation, but, the commander hastened to inform the Secretary of the Navy, the boy continued to be *"touched by the gentle and untiring attentions of Mr. Gansevoort."*

Mackenzie's alarm, temporarily allayed by his own address to his crew, was reviving again, and, once more, spreading to infect his officers. None was more responsive to the commander's fears than James W. Wales, although his disclosure of Spencer's plot already had paid off handsomely. Wales had been advanced temporarily to midshipman's rank in his victim's place and had received hints from the *Somers'* grateful captain of larger, more permanent reward.

Nevertheless, the erstwhile purser's steward seems to have been unhappy in his loftier berth, possibly because of an uneasy conscience. After Spencer, Cromwell, and Small had been turned about, the temporary midshipman came in haste to Gansevoort and panted a frightful tale.

The shackled Spencer, though his position lately had been reversed, still sat close to the arms chest and had managed to get a battle-ax from its rack. He was weighing it in his manacled hands and had cast backward toward his betrayer a look of such deadly, if explicable, animosity that Wales had not dared to go near the prisoner.

Spencer surrendered the weapon readily enough when the lieutenant approached him. In the hands of a man so weighted down by irons that he could not rise unaided, even the sharpest battle-ax was a dubious menace. Meek obedience did not lessen Mackenzie's belief that Spencer had armed himself in expectation of immediate rescue.

That word, that possibility, clung vampirelike to the minds of all the *Somers'* officers. It did not relax its depleting hold until Spencer, Cromwell, and Small had been placed beyond the possibility of mortal rescue. Contrary reasoning processes of frightened men arrived at dire, identical conclusion.

Thus, Gansevoort was certain that an attempt to free the prisoners was close at hand because Spencer had glared menacingly at Wales and had weighed a battle-ax. Sailing Master Perry believed mutinous rescue was near because the manner of the prisoners, during their confinement, *"appeared to be perfectly easy."*

At the time of their arrests, Mackenzie had told Cromwell and Small as well as Spencer, that he intended to take them back to New York for trial. They had nothing immediate to fear—or so they thought—not knowing to what disreputable lengths fury-hounded men can be driven.

Tension aboard the *Somers* increased, this Monday afternoon, as the sun slid down the sky and the terror by night again crept out of the east and toward the brig. The volatile confidence Mackenzie had gained from his own oration long since had evaporated. He prepared to face once more the excruciating ordeal.

For long, black hours his officers would be obliged to stalk about the brig with eyes and ears strained for sign of mutiny's impending explosion. Their captain did what he could do to lessen their peril.

Mackenzie increased the strength of his nighttime patrols by ordering his subordinates henceforth to stand watch and watch. They were to hold to that rhythm—four hours on duty, four hours off—while the crisis endured. This not too onerous routine, common enough on merchant vessels, rapidly exhausted the stamina of young naval officers, or so their commander maintained. He told Mr. Upshur that from now on until the three men were hanged, he himself was on deck most of the time.

The captain of the *Somers*, as the night of November 28 drew near, adopted another and unusual protective device. He decreed that hereafter all enlisted personnel on deck, except for men and boys actively engaged in working the brig, must lie flat during the hours of darkness and so remain. Mackenzie had done all that he could, at the moment, to save his command.

Neither pride nor common sense restrained the *Somers*' officers from surrender to pervading yet generally sourceless

panic. Mackenzie had become its embodiment. He had raised
the wind that swung the weather-vane minds of his subordinates in a single direction. His growing distrust of the crew inspired his officers to suspect and fear it, too.

In the less than two days since Spencer's arrest, the brig's
commander had scared himself into believing that the enlisted
men and boys were displaying still graver indications of imminent mutiny. He did not list these symptoms in his report; he confessed that he was unable to do it. They were
"dark and portentous." They were *"like the lowering sky
presaging a tornado* [which] *a seaman's eye could detect and
appreciate but which a seaman's tongue cannot adequately
describe."*

The sailor-author was too modest. He did as well as anyone
could, considering the materials on hand.

By this Monday afternoon, the commander's apprehensive
thought processes were paralleling the peculiar reasoning of his
lieutenant. Gansevoort had believed that Spencer was planning mutiny and that Cromwell was concerned in the plot because, in his own opinion, they had looked as though they
might be. Mackenzie had grown certain that the earthquake
fires of rebellion were about to erupt because of the appearance
of his crew.

If, as the commander maintained, the aspect of his men was
beyond a seaman's descriptive powers, that may have been because there was nothing much to describe, over and above an
unspecified *"sullenness."* Mackenzie could not report that he
had become unbearably terrified for no plain cause yet still
make the confession sound firmly courageous.

Darkness leaped like a great black cat upon the *Somers*.
Heavily armed officers resumed their patrol of perilous areas

where shadows promised ambush and moonlight had the glitter of bared steel. The sentries' progress was hampered by the many prone bodies they were obliged to avoid or step over.

Monday crept slowly to its end. During its tortuous passage, no mutinous word had been spoken, no mutinous act attempted.

CHAPTER 9

Tuesday, November 29

"The conspiracy, confident in its strength, matured in its counsels and murderous in its resolves, was now ripe for action."—ALEXANDER SLIDELL MACKENZIE.

THE WEATHER remained sardonically serene. The sunrise was golden and cloudless, yet its brilliance could not lighten the minds of men who lately had endured the long night's ordeal. The trade wind strained the *Somers'* canvas.

Her crew went about the first duties of the day with a docility that the brig's officers still found ominous. Forthright explosion might be easier to face than continuation of this foreboding composure.

Mackenzie surveyed his command closely as it mustered for morning quarters. Nothing perceptible had altered during the dark, depleting hours, except the aspect of one of the prisoners. The commander's eye seized and dwelt approvingly upon that single change.

The three captives squatted on the tail of the quarter-deck, still facing aft. Cromwell's great bulk minimized his irons, but Small seemed crushed by his. Mackenzie looked longest at Philip Spencer.

The boy sat alongside the larboard arms chest in a wretched, perhaps even a repentant, attitude. His boat cloak had been placed about him by the femininely attentive Gansevoort. Spencer's head was bent forward on his knees. The commander thought, with a literary man's intuition, that resistance had gone out of his principal captive. He sent his lieutenant to investigate.

"*Sir*," Gansevoort reported when he came back from his inquiry, "*Mr. Spencer's face is bathed in tears.*"

"*Indeed?*" Mackenzie asked with satisfaction.

Stoppage of the captives' tobacco already was unmanning one of the deprived. It might be well, later, to determine whether the tearful Mr. Spencer was ready to talk with less than that irksome self-possession he had maintained when arrested. In his present shattered state his tone might be gratifyingly contrite.

After muster, the commander would send the useful Mr. Gansevoort to sound out the chief suspect. If his mood proved to be truly promising, the lieutenant, like an envoy to a foreign power, might arrange for an interview between Mr. Spencer and the captain of the *Somers*.

Meanwhile, the crew had been mustered. When inspection had ended, Mackenzie saw to it that the wretched Waltham again was flogged thoroughly. Then, with Gansevoort's encouragement, he determined to address the brig's company once more. Oratory might relieve the commander's oppressed spirit, might recapture for him yesterday's evanescent belief that the *Somers* was safe.

Mackenzie's eloquence was muted by worry and sleeplessness. Besides, he chose this morning a less edifying topic. On Monday, he had dwelt upon the tear-starting theme of Home and Friends. Today, he dilated upon Crime and Punishment.

"*I again spoke to the crew, urging them to conform to the discipline of the vessel. The orders were all known and of easy observance. I mentioned that every punishment inflicted must be known to the secretary of the navy and that the less pun-*

*ishment there was, the more creditable it would be to the com-
mander and her crew."*

Mackenzie felt, when he had ended, that this had not been
one of his better achievements. His audience had not been re-
sponsive. Plainly, *"the whole crew was far from tranquillized."*
Something further must be done to save the imperiled brig.
The commander sent Plenipotentiary Gansevoort to sound out
Philip Spencer.

The interview was a semifailure. The boy hid his face in his
cloak, and his muffled voice was unsteady. Though in great distress, the prisoner clung to his pride. He was in no condition,
he told the emissary, to talk with anyone now. Tomorrow he
would have hold of himself again; tomorrow he would willingly answer whatever questions Commander Mackenzie
chose to ask.

Gansevoort, withdrawing, was smitten by a sudden and
novel thought. He paused beside the dismal Small. Perhaps, if
the little man were questioned, tactfully and delicately, he
might disclose something that would lessen the pervading
dread. It was worth a trial. The lieutenant cleared his throat.

"Small," he ventured, *"are there any men forward whom we
should have reason to fear?"*

Gansevoort was a halfhearted examiner. The conversation,
as he himself reported it, was lamed by mutual timidity. The
lieutenant's inquiries were hesitant, as though he feared forthright questioning might uncover too much. Small, naturally
unwilling to make his own plight worse, was wary in his replies.
Together they skittered over the surface of the crisis and never
got beneath it.

"Reason to fear, sir?" the little seaman echoed. *"Well now.
Mr. Gansevoort, that's a hard thing to say."*

The lieutenant fortified himself and dropped his voice, lest it carry to the manacled giant across the quarter-deck.

"Small, tell me: is not Cromwell engaged in this plot with Mr. Spencer?"

"And that's a hard thing to say, Mr. Gansevoort, sir," Small repeated, feeling his way. *"Real intimate, they've been. I've seen Mr. Spencer give him more money than I would like to give him—or lend him, either."*

He paused, unwilling to sell out for no discernible reward. Gansevoort summoned all his resolution:

"That is not the thing. I want a plain answer to a plain question. Is not Cromwell deeply engaged with Mr. Spencer to take the vessel out of the hands of her officers?"

He waited, scarcely breathing. After hesitation, the prisoner muttered, according to the lieutenant:

"Sir, if anyone on board is, Cromwell is."

"I thought so!" Gansevoort exclaimed and tiptoed away, well satisfied with his equivocal trove. He had obtained a moderate endorsement of his own suspicions, which seems to have been all his sensitive spirit could stand.

It was reasonably evident that Small, if encouraged, would have told all he knew—little or much—of Spencer's plot. He was questioned no further until a noose dangled above him.

On this morning of Tuesday, November 29, it was Gansevoort, not the prisoner, who closed the interview, while innumerable other important questions remained unuttered. That peculiar modesty which impelled all the brig's officers to shrink from unclad verity restrained the lieutenant from further examination of a suspect not unwilling to talk.

Gansevoort returned to Mackenzie and reported the outcome of a sketchy and spineless interview. The commander did not go and finish the job his first officer had botched. Instead, he accepted uncritically the lieutenant's fragmentary findings and discerned in them, precipitately, confirmation of his own belief that full-statured revolt was on the verge of eruption.

That conviction sent Mackenzie's mind scurrying away like a frightened rabbit from the path a more courageous man would have followed. The commander might have interviewed Small personally; he might even have summoned all his fortitude and have interviewed Cromwell. There is no evidence that, at any time between his arrest and death, the big boatswain ever was questioned by anyone.

After days of evasion and multiplying fright, Mackenzie had got himself into a mental state that made him recoil from forthright action of any variety. So he himself did not examine any of the prisoners. Instead, he ordered Gansevoort not to press Small further, but to move surreptitiously about the brig and see what he could pick up by eavesdropping.

The lieutenant reassumed his role of roving detective. From his hesitant prying, he gained little to hearten him. He considered that the aspect and behavior of the crew was far from normal. Steeling himself to more direct investigation, Gansevoort approached several of the petty officers, choosing those whom he believed most likely to be loyal. His hesitant conversations with these sent his own heart lower still.

Later in the day, the lieutenant returned from his sleuthing and reported to Mackenzie. Gansevoort's own observations and his interviews with the petty officers had convinced him that the brig was in graver peril.

The dazzling, uneventful hours passed. Men and boys performed their duties without any lapse that warranted citation in the logbook. The watches changed smoothly. Only a single untoward incident marred the rest of the day. Officers who had

watched vainly for anything that would justify their unsub-
dued fears seized upon this trifle and built it up beyond recognition.

The jumpy Temporary Midshipman Wales again was involved, this time with Seaman Charles A. Wilson who was
listed in the Greek Paper as likely to join the mutiny. Wales,
that afternoon, ran up to Mackenzie and reported breathlessly
that he had seen Wilson take a handspike from the brig's
launch.

The lately promoted steward panted further that he was certain Wilson intended to brain him. Wales had valiantly leveled his pistol and ordered the man to replace the handspike.
Wilson had obeyed with *"a lame excuse"* and then moved
away.

To minds less starved for material that would excuse a
chronic, pervasive terror, the incident would have been mean-
ingless. Mackenzie and his jackal did their best to enlarge it
into a barely averted murderous assault and the prelude to
open mutiny.

Wales was on the starboard side of the quarter-deck; Wilson, on the larboard, at the stern of the launch. The distance
between the men was about forty feet. If the reputed assailant
intended to crack an armed man's skull from so far away, the
length of his reach must have been even greater than the extent of Wales's apprehensions. On provender such as this, the
officers of the *Somers* fed their fears.

Facts, to which Mackenzie and his subordinates were becoming still more blind, fail to produce any definite instance
of disorder or disobedience on this, the next to the last day in
the lives of Spencer, Cromwell, and Small. The commander,
in his report, did his literary best to steep this actually unevent-

ful Tuesday in growing danger, but even his accomplished pen failed him here. It described apprehensions and presumptions, not proven instances of mutiny.

Mackenzie became convinced that the crew was far from tranquillized after his morning address and just possibly because of it. Gansevoort, with his customary misidentification of personal impressions as valid evidence, concluded that the enlisted personnel of the *Somers* was ripe for mutiny because to his eagle eye it looked as though it were.

In the light of what had already happened, it is hard to imagine how any crew's behavior could have remained normal. The erraticisms and aberrations of the brig's officers were bound to disturb their underlings.

Gentlemen of the wardroom and the steerage, heavily armed and taut as animal trainers among their beasts, prowled about the *Somers* and glowered at all and sundry. This was not empty display either. Pistols were being leveled on slight provocation, and one of them had been fired, however accidentally. Already a popular midshipman, a boatswain, and a seaman had been arrested for obscure offenses. Their exposure on the quarter-deck was a constant reminder that others at any moment might be surrounded, seized, and ironed, for reasons no clearer.

The crew were apprehensive—for cause. Mackenzie reported their nervousness as a dire portent.

"The most seriously implicated once more began to collect in knots . . . and an insolent and menacing air [was] *assumed by all."*

So the commander assured Mr. Upshur. Mackenzie never hinted, and quite probably he never admitted to his most secret self, that his own highly contagious terror was spreading to afflict his entire command. He swallowed uncritically the impressions Gansevoort brought back from his prying, peering

tour of the brig, though the only specific information he produced was the belief of certain petty officers that the *Somers*
was indeed in danger.

This was opinion; nothing more was elicited, and it is quite
likely that the petty officers were swayed by Gansevoort's own
agitation. In any event, they were on a spot. They could agree
with a superior, or else.

Boatswain's mates, gunner's mates, and the like did not
laugh at a lieutenant's fears. They dared not meet his questions
with a forthright:

"Come, come, Mr. Gansevoort, pull yourself together. If it's
suspicious behavior you're looking for, sir, consider your own."

If the brig's first officer believed that a mutiny was brewing
and rescue of the prisoners was about to be attempted, a man
who valued his berth had little choice. In the navy, you didn't
contradict a superior, particularly when such dispute might
win the disputant a set of irons.

Beyond the hollow omens in Gansevoort's report and the allegedly contemplated long-range assault upon Wales, even the
inventive pen of Alexander Slidell Mackenzie could set down
in the narrative of this day nothing to extenuate the dreadfulness that was to follow.

The afternoon wore away. Sunlight gilded the bellies of the
brig's sails. She still trampled evenly through the waves. The
first dog watch, however "*insolent and menacing*" its aspect,
had mustered without reportable disobedience or disorder, yet
Mackenzie was more alarmed. By the fright transference prev-
alent aboard the *Somers*, his officers were more frightened, too.

Another night of jeopardy and tension was drawing near.
How many more of these dark, protracted torments could men
endure and not go mad? The commander's eyes strayed over

his outwardly shipshape command and came to rest upon the backs of the three prisoners at the brig's stern. He stared at the submissive figures with a new, still more virulent detestation.

The captives were the sources of the evil; they were the focal points of the infection that was polluting his command. At length and with difficulty the captain of the *Somers* pulled his eyes away from the three meek and burdened figures and girded his spirit to withstand another night.

The sailor-author extended himself in describing for the benefit of the Secretary of the Navy the menaces and horrors that infested the last dire hours of that day, yet this section of his report is distinguished less for literary elegance than for a wild irresponsibility. He limited himself to awesome general statements, yet submitted no trace of evidence to support the most flagrant of them.

"*During the night,*" he informed Mr. Upshur, "*seditious words were heard throughout the vessel.*"

He quoted no such utterances, attributed them to no one, neglected to report who heard them.

"*Various intelligence was obtained from time to time of conferences among the disaffected.*"

Mackenzie did not say who obtained the intelligence or why his armed patrolling officers permitted the conferences.

"*Individuals, not before supposed to be very deeply implicated, now were found in close association with those who were.*"

The commander did not name the hitherto slightly implicated men; nor did he explain who saw these "*close associations.*"

"*Several times during the night, there were symptoms of an intention to strike some blow.*"

The report describes no symptom, disregards the natures of the contemplated blows.

"I could not contemplate this growth of disaffection without serious uneasiness. Where was this thing to end?"

The question was rhetorical—and hypocritical. By now, Alexander Slidell Mackenzie and his lieutenant had looked forward distractedly to the end. On Tuesday, November 29, they had agreed that Philip Spencer, Elisha Small, and Samuel Cromwell must be destroyed.

Gansevoort had discussed the idea with several officers—Sailing Master Perry, Midshipman Hays, and Dr. Leecock, among them—and had got at least majority approval. The project, originally advanced as a possibility, had acquired, before Tuesday ended, the aspect of immediate necessity. The lieutenant submitted it to the hagridden Mackenzie, who implicitly agreed.

No stark emergency, no mutinous explosion twisted the minds of the *Somers'* officers toward slaughter. Fright, pestilential and cumulative, impelled them. Dignity long ago had deserted Mackenzie and his young gentlemen. Now, decency was flaking away under the torment of waiting for an uprising that hung in the distance and refused to draw nearer.

The reasons the executioners advanced for hanging three shipmates were the invalid excuses of badly frightened men. Neither Spencer, nor Cromwell, nor Small, after arrest, had complicated in any degree his original offense. The guilt of the three men was no more evident now than it had been earlier when Mackenzie had informed each of them that he would be taken back to the United States for trial.

The prisoners were manacled, helpless, entirely subject to their captors, yet, to the dilated eyes of the *Somers'* officers, they radiated an awful menace that was becoming unbearable.

Mackenzie and his subordinates had been jostled onward by an omnivorous terror that made portents out of inconsequences and saw looming perils in trivialities.

Bit by bit, once upright men had been stripped of their integrity until now they considered what was in essence murder, no longer with revulsion, but as relief from what had become unendurable pressure.

The decision to hang the three captives was not predicated upon any recognized process of law. It was an emotional explosion. Mackenzie and his officers, having frightened themselves unbearably, turned upon the apparent source of the degrading dread with the same wild revulsion they might have displayed in crushing a spider or trampling on a snake. They did not recoil from what they were about to do; they looked beyond it to the relief that would be theirs when the thing had been accomplished.

The dark brig drove on through dimly shining seas. Men and boys not occupied with her progress lay, by their captain's order, prostrate on the deck. Armed officers, ceaselessly patrolling, moved tautly among them.

"*I felt more anxious than I yet had done,*" Mackenzie's report reads, "*and remained continually on deck.*"

In this, at least, there is a ring of truth.

The bell was rung eight times. The watches changed. A new day had overtaken the brig. That concluded had seen aboard her no proved mutinous deed or word.

CHAPTER 10

Wednesday, November 30

"To condemn a man out of his own mouth is a rule of evidence which the Judge of all the earth has condescended to inform us He will Himself adopt."—ALEXANDER SLIDELL MACKENZIE.

UNSETTLED MINDS were still wobbling. Certain officers of the *Somers* had discussed the killing of Spencer, Cromwell, Small. They had agreed it should be undertaken, yet a remaining vestige of sobriety made them hesitate.

The hanging of the prisoners without further provocation would resemble, not too coincidentally, a lynching. Since their arrest, the hyperperceptive vision of Mackenzie had discerned among his captives further evidence of guilt. His findings had been inspirational and limited to Spencer. The brig's officers needed a more substantial warrant for putting three men to death. They had no great difficulty in finding it.

The presence of the ironed prisoners on the quarter-deck was hampering the efficient working of the *Somers*. Obviously, then, if more were arrested and added to the original trio, they would obstruct navigation still further, enlarge the opportunities for rescue, increase the general peril. The officers modified their contention. They decided that if—and only if—more prisoners had to be taken, Spencer, Cromwell, and Small should hang.

This recommendation by gentlemen of the quarter-deck armed their captain against the formless terror that had been overwhelming him. The heartening weight of the new weapon forbade him to debate whether it was fair or foul. He had obtained sanction, however dubious, to strike back against those whom he considered the authors of his ordeal. He prepared to take more prisoners and destroy the earlier ones.

The three first captives and his frantic misapprehensions concerning them had so reduced a well-known naval officer and literary light that, weeks later, he could not describe coherently his emotional state at this moment.

"The deep sense I had," he informed Mr. Upshur, *"of the solemn obligation I was under to protect and defend the vessel that had been entrusted to me, and the lives of the officers and the crew—the seas traversed by our peaceful merchantmen and the unarmed of all nations using the highways of the seas from the horrors which the conspirators had meditated and, above all, to guard from violation the sanctity of the American flag* [The commander wrapped himself in the national ensign as habitually as he put on his nightshirt.] *all impressed on me the absolute necessity of adopting some further measures for the security of the vessel."*

Mackenzie proceeded on this Wednesday morning to adopt such measures. He hurriedly yet cannily prepared the stage for the final act of the tragedy. It seemed a propitious time. During the first minutes of this day, he himself had observed an irregularity, susceptible to the usual misinterpretation.

The commander had been on deck when the watches had changed at midnight. He had seen, with an immediate reading of dark significance into the lapse, that Daniel McKinley, still at large though certified as an enlisted mutineer by the Greek Paper, Benjamin F. Green, *"and others seriously implicated,"* had been late in mustering.

Mackenzie seized on this tardiness and embellished it without conscience:

"That they should have been asleep at all that night was unlikely. . . . There was probably an agreement to meet around the officer of the deck and commit some violence."

He immediately added this defection to his accumulated excuses for hanging three men and did not consider it worthy of mention that, according to the delinquent's own explanation, Alexander Slidell Mackenzie had been indirectly responsible for Daniel McKinley's apparent slackness.

The man and Alexander McKee *"turned in and out with one another,"* one going off watch as the other came on. Throughout the cruise, they had had a working agreement whereby each woke the other when his watch was mustered. In this particular instance, McKee had failed to rouse McKinley, who had overslept.

"I asked McKee why he did not call me. He told me the officers would not let him stir; that they were ordered to lie down on the deck and when he lay down he fell asleep and did not wake up. That was why I missed my muster, being used to be awaked by one another."

This was plausible enough, but Mackenzie would have none of it. He was immune by now to simple explanations. The commander immediately promoted McKinley to first place in the still-delayed mutiny.

Spencer, originally, had been accepted as the mutineer-in-chief. Mackenzie now discovered that McKinley, who, before enlistment, had been conditioned for a piratical career by employment as a waiter in Howard's Hotel, New York, was *"in fact the individual who, if the mutiny had been accomplished, would have made away with all his competitors and then risen to command."*

How the commander arrived at this conclusion is not clear. If his reasoning was frequently obscure, it was always filled with surprises.

This far from sinister incident inspired Mackenzie to gloomy literary reflections for the benefit of Mr. Upshur and posterity:

"If the most deeply implicated of the crew were ironed, would all the dangerous be in custody? What sympathy might not be inspired by the suffering of the prisoners?"

Again, the inquiry is shabby rhetoric. He was already preparing to impose upon three prisoners the extremity of suffering. Before morning muster, the commander had gone below to his cabin and there had composed a singular letter to his principal subordinate officers. He somewhat unnecessarily had called their attention to the fact that three men had been arrested for mutiny. He also had written of *"disaffection"* among the crew and then had pursued with more than usual turgidity:

"Knowing that suspicions of the gravest nature attach to persons still at large, and whom the difficulty of taking care of the prisoners we already have makes me more reluctant than I otherwise should be to apprehend, I have determined to address myself to you and ask your united counsel as to the best course to be now pursued, and I call upon you to take into deliberate and dispassionate consideration the present condition of the vessel and the contingencies of every nature that the future may embrace, throughout the remainder of our cruise, and enlighten me with your opinion as to the best course to be pursued."

The commander signed this communication and addressed it to Lieutenant Gansevoort, Purser Heiskill, Dr. Leecock, Sailing Master Perry, Midshipmen Rogers, Thompson, and Hays. Then he laid it aside for future use.

Alexander Slidell Mackenzie was not at his most attractive

while composing this singular letter. On its surface, it was strange enough, being an appeal for advice on how to behave, addressed to his subordinates by the captain of a United States man-of-war. The missive had obvious structural and less apparent moral defects. It was at once hypocritical and homicidal.

Apart from his maltreatment of the English language, the commander was exquisitely careful in framing this communication. He and some of his officers already had agreed that, if more prisoners were taken, the first three should be put to death. There was no least reference to hangings in the letter, yet its author felt certain of his subordinates' responsive verdict. His appeal for guidance was pretense. He was deftly imposing upon his officers at least part of the responsibility for the contemplated executions.

There was a revolting alacrity in Mackenzie's subsequent movements. He left the letter on his desk and prepared to expedite the execution of Spencer, Cromwell, and Small by arresting further suspects.

The crew had been mustered when their captain reached the quarter-deck. He assumed command, assembled a force of commissioned and petty officers, and seized four more men.

One by one, as the commander called their names, Wilson, McKinley, Green, and McKee were hauled out of formation and frog-marched to where Mackenzie and Gansevoort stood with pistols cocked and poised and Henry King, gunner, flourished a handspike. None of the cat-and-mouse suavity that had distinguished Spencer's arrest was present now. The activity was panicky and brutal. McKinley remembered his experience thus:

"The commander cried: 'Send McKinley aft.' I went aft.

*The commander and Mr. Gansevoort held pistols at my head
and told me to sit down. Mr. Gansevoort told King, the gunner, to stand by to knock their brains out if they should make
a false motion. I was put in irons. . . . Mr. Gansevoort ordered
me to get on all fours and creep round to the larboard side,
as I could not walk."*

This raw ferocity may have been due to long overstrained
nerves. If the manhandled captives, the leveled pistols, the
threats, the clanking irons were adopted to awe a reputedly
disaffected crew, the display was successful; it may even have
been entirely unnecessary.

Throughout the panicky episode, which might well have
incited prospective mutineers to revolt, men and boys rigidly
kept formation. The furore indicates how greatly discipline
had fallen off among the officers, not the crew, of the *Somers*
within the last few days.

The muster's orderly appearance gave Mackenzie no further
opportunity to terrify himself. Indeed, the aspect of his command seemed so docile that with Gansevoort closely in reserve
he ventured to move along the lines of seamen and apprentices
and even to question some of them. In this enterprise Commander Alexander Slidell Mackenzie, U.S.N., by his own report, was timorously selective:

*"I walked deliberately around the battery, followed by the
first lieutenant, and we made a very careful inspection of the
crew. Those who (though known to be very guilty) were
considered the least dangerous, were called out and interro-
gated.*

*"Care was taken not to awaken the suspicions of such as
from courage and energy were really formidable."*

When the hazardous inspection had been completed without offense to the really formidable, muster was dismissed.

The first step toward the hangings had been safely executed. Mackenzie now could serve his already prepared and implicitly expediting letter upon his senior subordinates.

The commander turned to go below, and then paused, staring at a possible source of damning evidence. Philip Spencer seemed more composed this morning. He had offered to answer today any questions Mackenzie cared to ask. It might be well, the commander reflected, to see what hanging material he could get from the boy—not personally, of course, but with Mr. Gansevoort as intermediary. Pending the result of such inquiry, it would be best to let the letter wait.

The lieutenant's interview with Spencer was trite and superficial. The prisoner answered questions readily, but Gansevoort was a reluctant investigator. He may have felt that he was doing a specially dirty job. He and others had recommended that, if more prisoners were taken, the first three should be killed. There were seven captives on the quarterdeck now, and Gansevoort had been detailed to implicate further a doomed man.

Spencer, still sustained by Mackenzie's earlier promise that he would be taken home for trial, had himself under better control this morning, though he looked *"a little more melancholy and gloomy than usual."* According to Gansevoort, the boy frankly admitted that he had dabbled in mutiny.

"He said he had had this plot aboard every vessel he had been in; had it on the Potomac *and* John Adams *but never had got so far with it as he had aboard the* Somers. *He said he knew it would get him into trouble. He had thought it over in the steerage and had tried to break himself of it, but could not. He thought it was a mania with him."*

That thought may have been a fairer judgment than any other, defensive or accusatory, that has been visited upon the boy.

The conversation was suspended here while Gansevoort hurried away, to return with Acting Midshipman Deslonde and the cipher. The prisoner identified the Greek Paper and admitted that he had compiled it. At the lieutenant's request, he interpreted while Deslonde wrote down his words. Spencer's translation was identical with Midshipman Rogers' earlier. When the prisoner had completed it, his interviewer could think of only one more question to ask:

Did not the name "E. Andrews," in the roster of those considered certain mutineers, stand for Cromwell? Spencer shook his head.

"No, sir. It stands for Small. That is his real name."

"How can it stand for Small," Gansevoort returned astutely, "when you have Small's name entered twice, elsewhere in the list?"

"Oh!" Spencer said and paused in apparent surprise. "I didn't know I had written it in that way."

That was the extent of the lieutenant's investigation. It was broken off here, for no clear reason. This interrogation, feeble and faltering, was the sole opportunity to defend himself granted Philip Spencer before he was sentenced to be hanged. It was the sleazy travesty of his rightful day in court.

Mackenzie received his lieutenant's report of the interview, bustled down into his cabin, returned with the letter he had written hours earlier, and formally delivered it to Gansevoort.

The trade wind sang. The brig, under studding sails, sliced through the water so blue that it bleached the sky. Patches of golden Sargasso weed slid past. The Somers was nearing the end of her long reach west and north from Africa. She was crossing the doorstep of the island-strewn Caribbean. St. Thomas, her destination, still was distant, but the broadcast crumbs of land that are the Lesser Antilles—Barbados, Dominica, Guadeloupe, St. Lucia, and the rest—were not far beyond the horizon. Antigua, the nearest, was some sixty hours' sailing time away, but there was a frenzied urgency aboard the brig that forbade men to wait for a landfall and the relief from terror that it promised.

In the wardroom, the *Somers'* senior officers were assembling to consider the problem embodied in Mackenzie's letter. On deck, the crew, less its captive members, had recovered whatever balance it had lost during the panicky process of taking more prisoners and the commander's subsequent faltering inquisition. Men and boys, said to be seething with mutiny, had resumed their duties, under no more official control than Mackenzie and three junior midshipmen—Tillotson, Deslonde, and O. H. Perry—could exert.

While the council of officers below began to measure the dimensions of the alleged conspiracy, there was eloquent denial topside that any plot existed other than in their own roiled minds. The commander, by taking the deck himself with no support but three young boys, had offered mutineers a unique opportunity to revolt. Mackenzie's principal subordinates were out of immediate reach if trouble should start. Hour after hour went by tamely without a single untoward incident that the captain of the *Somers* deemed worth recording.

The fresh breeze lifted the brig along; her wake spun out the miles; yet, during this long interval while she was extraordinarily vulnerable, a crew outnumbering the officers present by twenty-five to one obeyed orders. Save for the clutter of prisoners on the quarter-deck, all seemed normal and serene. It was otherwise below. In the wardroom disgraceful things were being done by the officers' council, assembled at Mackenzie's behest. He, himself, half-apologized later for some of that gathering's deficiencies.

The council, its creator explained, with an odd blending of regret and complacence, was an unconventional body, born of emergency. It may have had defects, but it also had one uncommon virtue, derived from Alexander Slidell Mackenzie's own fortunate possession which, being of divine origin, obviously made everything else all right.

"Under these circumstances, what was the commander of the Somers to do? He was alone on the ocean.... The high seas furnished no learned jurists with whom he might consult but he had with him a volume of nature's laws, written by the finger of God on the human heart. In that volume he read that necessity ordains its own controlling canons."

Though he and his officers had been guided by this ineffable script, the commander wished it distinctly understood that the legal proprieties were observed.

"On the receipt of my letter, the officers immediately assembled in the wardroom and commenced the examination of witnesses. The witnesses were duly sworn and the testimony accurately written down. In addition to the oath, each witness signed the evidence he had given, after it had been read over to him."

The council was less respectable, infinitely less competent, scandalously less decent than the commander maintained. In the overcrowded wardroom, officers who had expressed the belief that Spencer, Cromwell, and Small should be hanged scrabbled frantically and lawlessly to find material that would shore up their already uttered verdict. They undertook a more grisly Alice-in-Wonderland proceeding; they ran their trial backward and, reeling still further into legal absurdity, conducted it in the absence of the defendants.

Mackenzie's heart-bound testament of *"nature's laws"* ignored the first and most essential of human statutes. Nothing in the commander's report to Secretary Upshur, nothing in his other elaborate self-defenses, indicates that the marine kangaroo court he established ever gave even fleeting consideration to the fundamental right of men on trial for their lives. The officers' council made no effort to bring the accused before the accusers. It never examined the three prisoners or let them know what was happening to them. Not until they were about to die were Spencer, Cromwell, and Small informed that they had been tried, judged, condemned.

The intentions and the proceedings of the council were equally disreputable. It chose as secretary Purser Heiskill, who discharged his duties in an unrestrained and original fashion. Then, having ventured so far and no further toward formality, the body adopted a go-as-you-please policy with no one in charge, no one objecting to this omission, and frequently with two or three persons asking questions at the same time. Witnesses were haled into this hurly-burly and were examined from several directions at once with startling results.

It is questionable whether any attempt by seven lawyers to navigate the *Somers* could have resulted in a more calamitous mess than this effort of seven naval officers to hold a legal examination. All the competent evidence obtained need not have taken fifteen minutes to produce, yet the council stumbled, fumbled, came up with many irrelevances and outrages, and continued in session till darkness fell. It adjourned then, reconvened the next morning, and continued to stew for several hours before it reached a decision.

Thirteen witnesses appeared before the body. There is no

indication how this sketchy sampling of the entire crew was made or whether any statement by any of these persons was rejected. It was James Fenimore Cooper's opinion that:

"*A more precious set of depositions was probably never flouted in the face of justice. Nine-tenths of their matter would be rejected in the loosest court in Christendom.*"

The assertions by witnesses, incompetent enough in their original state, were amended by the secretary, edited, and, in one instance at least, embellished by deliberate forgery. The slippery Mr. Heiskill recorded the testimony of George W. Warner, which contained nothing more evidential than his own highly derogatory opinion of Cromwell. The secretary then appended to the deposition the following:

Q. "*What was your reason for saying to Green: 'The damned son of a bitch (meaning Cromwell) ought to be hung'?*"

A. "*Because I thought him guilty.*"

That isn't the way Great-uncle George told it. He wrote his own version of his appearance before the council, while he was still jailed aboard the *North Carolina*. By then, his detestation of all things naval seems to have been well advanced. He described aggrievedly the confusion in the wardroom, where each officer considered himself an examiner and all talked at once.

"*Before,*" young Warner complained, "*a question of one officer was answered, others would be put by other officers, thus not only confounding the person being examined but themselves.*"

After spending considerable scorn and space upon Purser-Secretary Heiskill and his original method of deposition-taking, my ancestor voiced his principal indignation:

"*As an indication of the correctness of the so-called 'deposi-*

tions', I cite one instance. I was asked why I had said: 'If I had my way with the damned son of a bitch, Cromwell, I would hang him,' which had no answer. The question as put was not answered by me for the reason I had no answer to make to it. I hated Cromwell, and he me.

"The discovery was made by Purser Heiskill in making up a clean copy and he left a blank to be filled. He wanted me to fill in my answer. I answered that I had no answer to make. After some time spent to induce me to make an answer, which I did not, he said: 'Well, sign it and I will fill up the answer.' I signed and left the wardroom. He subsequently wrote in as my answer: 'Because I believe him guilty.' "

On deck, Mackenzie fumed and fidgeted. The council was taking an inordinate amount of time to arrive at a foregone conclusion. The delay was maddening, but he could do something to repair it. Long before his officers had reached a decision, the commander had arranged all the details for a triple hanging.

The captain of the *Somers* had leisure that outwardly uneventful afternoon to prepare a watch bill for the executions. While the brig ran smoothly and seven prisoners roosted on her stern, unaware that death was being contrived for three of them, Mackenzie wrote out the assignment of posts and duties for all on board. This was to be put into effect as soon as the inexplicably delayed but inevitable verdict of the council had been announced.

While so engaged, the captain of the *Somers* left the management of a supposedly rebellious crew in the hands of three green youngsters.

Below, in the lurching, overcrowded chamber, the beliefs of men rocked, too. The hearts of the council members had not been divinely inscribed, and nothing was happening to clarify foggy minds. The babblings of witnesses, however incompetent, irrelevant, immaterial, or downright nonsensical, were accepted and transcribed by Secretary Heiskill, after his peculiar fashion. The most nearly valid evidence was furnished by Mr. Wales, who submitted the first of his several written versions of his talk with Spencer.

The remainder of the testimony consisted almost entirely of hearsay and expressions of opinions, usually ridiculous. As recorded by the purser-secretary, some of it read:

Oliver P. Browning: "*I do not believe it safe to have Cromwell, Small and Spencer on board.... To tell you God Almighty's truth, I believe that some of the cooks around the galley, I think they are the main hackers—viz., Waltham, Cousin, Howard, Gallia. I have my suspicions also about some of the boys.*"

Thomas Dickinson: "*I think that the following persons still at large are concerned in it, viz., Kneavals, Golderman, Sullivan, Hamilton, Van Velsor, Whitmore, Garrabrantz, Godfrey (partly concerned in it) and Waltham, he more so than ever within two or three days. Thinks Mr. Spencer was at the head of the plan.*"

William Collins: "*Wishes Cromwell, Small and Spencer were out of the ship; thinks she would be more safe. Thinks that Spencer is the leader of the gang. Thinks that Cromwell is engaged in it. Heard him (Cromwell) say he had been in a slaver. Heard him tell the doctor this.*"

Andrew Anderson: "*From the first night Mr. Spencer was confined and from what I heard from my shipmates, I suspected they were plotting to take the vessel.... I don't know about the niggers in the galley. I don't like them. Cromwell could get anything from the galley. They appeared to like*

Cromwell there. He would very often take his pot and get coffee there."

Henry King: *"Thinks Cromwell the head man. Thinks they have been engaged in it ever since we left New York. Thinks if they could get adrift, there would be danger of the vessel being taken."*

Charles Stewart: *"I don't think the vessel is safe with these prisoners aboard. This is my deliberate opinion from what I heard King, the gunner's-mate say; that is, that he had heard the boys say there were spies about."*

These witnesses were to have their reward, if Mackenzie could contrive it. He was willing to pay lavishly for worthless testimony. His report to Secretary Upshur later urged that Wales be promoted to purser, which would have jumped his pay from $18 a month to $1,500 a year. The commander also recommended that Collins, Browning, Stewart, King, Anderson, and Dickinson be advanced to warrant-officer rating, which would have raised their pay from $19 a month to $700 a year.

In the sweltering wardroom where everyone talked at once and Heiskill recorded the disorderly proceedings in his own unreliable fashion, hours passed without any perceptible progress toward a verdict. No man, save possibly the sensitive Dr. Leecock, seemed conscious of the ghastly quality of this ante-mortem burlesque.

Yet other officers belatedly may have become aware of it, and the council's procrastination may have been due to their sudden unwillingness to decree, openly and in their own version of legality, the deaths that they informally had urged. Mackenzie had thrust upon them responsibility that they may have been reluctant to assume.

They dawdled, whether purposefully or not, accepting trash

as evidence, interrupting each other, expressing their own opinions in the presence of witnesses, and questioning these in a
scrambled fashion that offered infinite opportunities for error.

Before the council had reached decision, Mackenzie's patience ran out. At twilight, he ordered the investigation to sus-
pend. Its members resumed the watch-and-watch ordeal of
protecting the brig against a menacing crew that, for part of
the afternoon, had been commanded by three boys.

Though four more suspects had been arrested and ironed on
this day, though three men were to be hanged for mutiny on
the morrow, no mutinous act had been observed, no mutinous
word spoken.

CHAPTER 11

Black Thursday

"In the necessities of my position, I found my law and in them also I must trust to find my justification."—ALEXANDER SLIDELL MACKENZIE.

THURSDAY'S MORNING muster had been dismissed. The seven officers who composed the suspended council had gone below to resume their investigation. Though nothing had happened since nightfall on Wednesday to indicate that the moment of mutiny was nearer, Mackenzie waited in increasing anxiety for word from the wardroom. It did not come.

The commander, neither a patient nor resolute man, had expected a prompt verdict the day before. He had prepared a watch bill for the hangings accordingly. Everything had been made ready for the execution, yet the enabling word continued to be withheld. Mackenzie found the delay bewildering and irritating. This novel reluctance of his subordinates to tell him in concert what several of them already had confided individually was a frustration that became intolerable as minutes collected into hours this radiant morning.

The captain of the *Somers* had determined to blast completely the discernible sources of the terror that infested his brig. Beside his material schedule for the conduct of the hangings, he had composed a second and psychic watch bill, outlining the sterling role he intended to play in the forthcoming, now tormentingly retarded, drama. Resolution must have wavered and the leading part he had assigned himself grown dim while he waited.

At length Mackenzie rebelled against further procrastination. He summoned Gansevoort from the wardroom, made acid inquiry, and sent the lieutenant back to his dilatory colleagues with a peremptory order to hurry.

The council still was having great difficulty in making up its collective mind. Members may have seen more clearly by now that their commanding officer had dumped into their laps the primary responsibility for absolving or hanging three men. If they did not condemn Spencer, Cromwell, and Small, such action would be counter to Mackenzie's implicit but obvious wishes and would do nothing to allay their own persistent fears.

On the other hand, if they decreed that the three men should die, they qualified as accessories to, if not instigators of, the killings. Recognition of that stark dilemma may have caused the hapless officers to postpone decision till the latest possible minute. The commander's message, relayed by Gansevoort, booted them forward.

Toward midmorning, the council had run out of witnesses, argument, and any further reasons for delay. It pulled itself together and proceeded to doom three men in a single, nonstop sentence, remarkable alike for length and incoherence:

"*Sir: In answer to your letter of yesterday, requesting our counsel as to the best course to be pursued with the prisoners, Acting Midshipman Philip Spencer, Boatswain's Mate Samuel Cromwell and Seaman Elisha Small, we would state that the evidence that has come to our knowledge is of such a nature as, after as dispassionate and deliberate a consideration of the case as the exigencies of the time would admit, we have come to a cool, decided and unanimous opinion that they have been guilty of a full and determined intention to commit a mutiny on board of this vessel of an atrocious nature and that the revelation of circumstances having made it necessary to confine others with them, the uncertainty as to what extent they are leagued with others still at large, the impossibility of guarding against the contingencies which 'a day or an hour may bring forth' we are convinced that it would be impossible to carry them to the United States, and that the safety of the public property, the lives of ourselves and of those committed to our charge require that (giving them sufficient time to prepare) they should be put to death, in a manner best calculated as an example to make a beneficial impression upon the disaffected.*

"This opinion [the council concluded, recovering breath] *we give, bearing in mind our duty to our God, our country and to the service. We are, sir* [they added in unconscious irony], *very respectfully your obedient servants."*

Mackenzie accepted the letter as a drowning man clutches a line.

"I at once concurred with the justice of this opinion and in the necessity for carrying it into immediate effect."

Thus, the commander wrote in his report to the Secretary of the Navy. Eight pages of that unique document's printed transcript cover significant happenings aboard the *Somers* from August 20, 1842, up to the morning of December 1. Mackenzie filled seven additional pages in describing the events of the subsequent twelve hours.

Until the sailor-author turned to the executions, he did not exhibit the entire dimensions of his literary talent. The reading public of that spiritually sticky era was gruesomely fascinated by accounts of the last words and acts of the expiring, and Alexander Slidell Mackenzie, the popular writer, did his best to oblige. He scrupulously observed and adorned with verbal arabesques every detail of an episode that most men in his position would have been eager to forget.

A young lieutenant had written in his *A Year in Spain*, Vol. I, p. 383, concerning a hanging he had witnessed in Madrid:

"Surely there can be nothing in such a spectacle to promote morality; nothing to make us either better or happier."

The captain of the *Somers*, by the testimony of his own pen, had come a long and not entirely admirable way since then.

With the pseudo warrant from his reluctant officers at last in hand, Mackenzie turned briskly to implementing it. None of the hesitation that lately had afflicted his subordinates, no sympathy for the men he was about to hang hampered the commander.

"The three chief conspirators alone were capable of navigating and sailing the brig. By their removal, the motive for a rescue, capture and carrying out of the original design of piracy at once was taken away. Their lives *were justly forfeited to the country and the honor and security of its flag* [there he goes again] *required that the sacrifice, however painful, should be made.*

"In the necessities of my position, I found my law and in them also I must trust to find my justification."

The red-haired commander with the delusive look of mildness thrust his officers' letter into his coat—each bit of supporting evidence must be carefully preserved henceforth—and applied himself to his long-prepared, long-delayed intention. Mackenzie addressed his lieutenant crisply:

"*Mr. Gansevoort, muster the petty officers on the quarter-deck at once. Issue to each of them cutlass, pistol, and cartridge box.*"

"*Ah—aye aye, sir.*"

This was directly contrary to all the intuitions of the faltering lieutenant, who had got himself into so extreme a state of apprehension that he distrusted most men. He was certain that all the petty officers were not loyal. Mackenzie, carried forward by a new confidence, ignored Gansevoort's perturbations. When the bewildered men had been duly armed, the commander addressed them with uncommon brevity:

"*My lads, you are to look to me, obey my orders, and see to it that my orders are obeyed. Go forward.*"

To Gansevoort, he said as the petty officers trooped away:

"*Pipe all hands aft to witness punishment.*"

Whistles shrilled; bawling voices amplified the order. With shuffling and a muted buzz of speech, the crew mustered. They took in their stride this unusual break in the day's routine. Men and boys had been exposed to so much irregularity in the last few days that this comparatively minor abnormality failed to excite them greatly. It seems to have been some time before they understood the final purpose of the orders their revitalized commander rapped out. They meekly obeyed them all, before and after comprehension.

Fierce sunlight fell upon the deck, and the shadows cast by sails and rigging swirled about the formation that broke apart smartly to execute Mackenzie's orders. Topmen, swarming aloft, furled the mainsail, then hauled three blocks up to the yardarm and lashed them there. Whips—light lines—were rove through the blocks and brought down to the deck again. Two dangled on the brig's starboard side; the other, to larboard.

In accordance with the watch bill he prematurely had composed on Wednesday, while the council was still wrangling,
Mackenzie stationed armed officers and petty officers at critical
posts about the deck. Thereafter, he completed his stage setting, with due regard for romantic proprieties.

"The afterguard and idlers of both watches were mustered
on the quarterdeck at the whip intended for Mr. Spencer; the
forecastle men and foretop men at that of Cromwell to whose
corruption they had been chiefly exposed; the maintop men of
both watches at that intended for Small, who for a month or
more had held the situation of captain of the maintop."

The national ensign had been bent on and was ready for
hoisting. Men were fashioning nooses at the whips' free ends.
Mackenzie and Gansevoort of the eagle eye surveyed the distributed crew. Each member was obediently in place. The
most dim-witted of the seamen and apprentices, strung along
the whips like animated beads, must have understood by now
his captain's purpose.

Three, perhaps all, of the prisoners who huddled on the
quarter-deck with their backs, by command, turned toward the
involved activity, were about to be hanged. This was the cru-
cial moment. The captain of the Somers at last had challenged
the "conspiracy." Suspected mutineers were to execute the
principal plotters.

No insubordinate voice was raised; no least act of rebellion
was attempted. A crew, believed to be thoroughly disaffected,
waited with oxlike patience for further orders. Its docility did
not bring disbelief in the existence of a plot to the commander's infatuated mind. He ordered his officers, commissioned or
petty, to cut down any man who released a whip with even one
hand. Then, with the scene satisfactorily set for the tragedy,
he prepared himself for his own leading role. Alexander Slidell

Mackenzie went down to his cabin and arrayed himself in his dress uniform.

Returning, he *"proceeded to execute the most painful duty that has ever devolved on an American commander—that of announcing to the criminals their fate."* Such duty seldom has been performed in a more feline fashion.

Sunlight smote the returning commander. It blazed upon epaulets, buttons, and gilt bindings as he paced toward the prisoners. Cromwell, better able than his companions to sustain the weight of his irons, sat on the starboard arms chest and read a copy of *The Penny Magazine.* The others, stupefied by heat, dozed or indifferently watched the wake of the brig measure the vessel's progress on what they all still believed was their voyage home.

The track foamed out beneath the stern's overhang and, running toward the horizon, was bent by wind and tide out of the straight line of the *Somers'* course. Beyond that white curve, sea and sky were no longer sharply joined. Haze that was forming into cloud had erased their meeting. A rain squall, if it overtook the brig, would revive the wilted captives. Meanwhile, drenched by the sun, they were conscious of little more than that misery shared by so many was easier to endure.

The glittering figure of Mackenzie intruded upon this apathetic company, and Daniel McKinley, blinking up at the unexpected splendor, believed for an instant that another vessel was in sight and that the commander had arrayed himself to visit her.

While the other prisoners gaped, Mackenzie stalked past them and confronted Spencer, who was perched upon the larboard arms chest. McKinley testified that the commander bluntly told the boy that he was to be executed in ten minutes and, when the captive babbled that he was not fit to die and begged for more time to compose himself, retorted:

"*I know you are not, but I cannot help it.*"

Such brevity was contrary to Mackenzie's nature. His version of the episode has no resemblance to McKinley's. It is unimportant which man lied. What the captain of the *Somers* said he said is sufficiently self-soiling, and he reported it fulsomely.

He may have set his speech down accurately; he may have fabricated it long afterward. In either event, he mercilessly assailed the defenseless boy whose crackbrained plot and the monstrous fears it had bred had brought the commander so low.

Mackenzie, according to his own report, dwelt gleefully on Spencer's offense. It had been the prisoner's intention to murder his captain "*in the darkness of night, in my sleep, without a moment to utter one murmur of affection to my wife and children, one prayer for their welfare.*"

Well, it hadn't worked out as it had been planned, the commander pursued triumphantly. It was Spencer, not his superior, who was going to die, but his executioner's intentions were more merciful than the boy's had been. Still according to his report, Mackenzie continued:

"*If there yet remains in you one feeling true to nature, it shall be gratified. If you have any word to send your parents, it shall be recorded and faithfully delivered. You have precisely ten minutes' leeway.*"

Mackenzie turned to Midshipman Thompson and bade him announce when ten minutes had elapsed. Then the commander observed with reportorial zeal the effect of his proclamation on his victim.

"He sank with tears upon his knees and said he was not fit to die. I repeated to him his own catechism and begged him at least to let the officer set to the men he had corrupted and seduced the example of dying with decorum."

Mackenzie was to stoop still lower in the next few hours. He turned now from the quaking boy and more curtly told the hulking Cromwell that he was about to be hanged. Here, too, the announcement was gratifyingly sensational. *The Penny Magazine* dropped from the prisoner's manacled hands. He tried to rise, rolled from the arms chest with a clash of irons, and, kneeling, bellowed:

"God of the Universe, look down upon my poor wife. I am innocent."

The glittering commander stood for a happy instant above the stricken giant, then recrossed the deck. The prisoners not yet approached watched his progress with sickened eyes. The purpose of the man in blue and flashing gold now was dreadfully plain to all.

Mackenzie halted before Small. The little man heard his doom with unexpected composure. No, he replied to the prompting question, he had no last words to send to anyone. He would prefer that his old mother should not know how her son had died.

It was not until after Spencer, Cromwell, and Small had been executed that Mackenzie was pleased to inform his remaining prisoners—McKee, Green, Wilson, and McKinley—that they were not to hang, too. He let them lie, coldly sweating, through the ensuing protracted emotional debauch. No doubt he considered this torment a proper part of their punishment.

McKinley admitted that he cried when he learned at last

that he was to live. Tears were appallingly plentiful on the brig
that day.

Spencer's eyes were fixed upon the commander. When Mackenzie returned to him, the boy reiterated the statement he
had made to Gansevoort days before.

"*As these are the last words I have to say,*" he said
earnestly, "*I trust they will be believed. Cromwell is innocent.*"

The statement, uttered in extremity, upset the commander's
balance. He admitted that he was "*staggered.*" He had made
all things ready for three hangings, yet his convictions were so
unstable that a single assertion had set them reeling.

Mackenzie left Spencer and sent for his lieutenant, that reliable prop for every wavering conviction. Mr. Gansevoort was
sure that there could be no doubt of Cromwell's guilt, but the
other, still groping, suggested that, to bolster the verdict of
the officers' council, the petty officers be asked for their opinion.

The lieutenant's evidence and his superior's report are not
in agreement on the result of this poll. Cromwell, the commander wrote, "*was condemned by acclamation by the petty
officers.*" Gansevoort, differing for once with his superior,
maintained that "*nobody said he* [Cromwell] *was innocent.*"
Mackenzie had no difficulty in turning a general negative into
a unanimous affirmative.

This highly original method of authorizing an execution,
this condemnation by acclamation, sent James Fenimore
Cooper into one of his louder uproars.

" 'By acclamation!' *What deeper disgrace can be attached to
our gallant navy than that, on board one of its vessels, the petty
officers were appealed to* viva-voce *in a question of life and*

death; and that, in obedience to their viva-voce *reply, the work of death went on!*

"*This simple admission by Commander Mackenzie should be sufficient to cashier him from the navy and cause that his commission and his sword and epaulettes be trodden under* [the] *foot of outraged justice as having suffered an unutterable, an irretrievable disgrace.*"

The commander, despite the petty officers' verdict, was still staggered. He shrank from the idea that anyone, even Philip Spencer, should uphold Cromwell's innocence. Mackenzie returned to the doomed boy, who had spoken so disturbingly in defense of a friend—or accomplice. Bending over Spencer, the captain of the *Somers* did his spiteful best to destroy that loyalty.

It was all very well, Mackenzie jeered, to say that Cromwell was guiltless, but that was nonsense and everyone knew it. The man had been using Spencer for his own ends, as the whole crew was aware. Some very nasty things had been said recently about Mr. Spencer, but perhaps he would rather not hear them.

The commander paused until the boy "*had expressed great anxiety to hear what was said,*" and then went on. Only recently, one of the petty officers had told Lieutenant Gansevoort:

"*In my opinion, sir, you have the damned fool on the larboard arms chest and the damned villain on the starboard.*"

And that, Mackenzie crowed, was by no means all. Another man had expressed the belief that, if the brig had been taken, Cromwell would have assumed command immediately. He might have allowed the demoted Spencer to live, if he had made himself useful—perhaps as the pirate chief's secretary.

"*I do not think,*" the commander gloated, "*this would have suited your temper.*"

He was gratified to find that "*this effectually aroused*" Spencer.

"*His countenance assumed a demoniac expression. He said no more of the innocence of Cromwell.*"

Long before Mackenzie had completed his spiteful tattling, the ten minutes he had allowed Philip Spencer had run out. Midshipman Thompson's announcement of this fact had gone unheeded. The commander was squandering time prodigally and, in the light of his earlier convictions, perilously.

Each minute's delay gave a reputedly mutinous crew further opportunity to revolt, more time to recover from the stupefaction of surprise. Delay invited the rebellious to rise up, overwhelm the loyal, release the prisoners, and capture the brig, yet no least instance of disorder was discerned by her officers.

In the entire muster, no man stirred from his station. No one displayed the most trivial insubordination during the long interval that was to elapse before another command was spoken.

The easily roused apprehensions of Mackenzie were running away with him—this time in another direction. The commander had sent to his cabin for pen, ink, paper, and a campstool. He had seated himself beside the arms chest where Philip Spencer squatted, and alternately was questioning him and furiously writing.

The commander was to remain in close conference with Spencer for an hour or more. The purpose of this long-delayed examination of the principal prisoner, what Mackenzie wrote, what he retained, what he may afterward have destroyed, never have been, never can be determined.

Defenders of Spencer have held that the boy either penned

or dictated a farewell letter to his parents that was never delivered. The commander insisted that every word set down during the interview was embodied in his report. To fortify this contention, he produced a page covered with disjointed and often illegible scribblings. An affidavit by Mackenzie accompanied these incoherencies. He deposed and swore that the page was *"the only memorandum or writing of any description made by him on that day while in communication with Mr. Spencer."*

There the question lies, yet will not rest.

The memorandum was so blind, so fragmentary that the doomed boy, rather than his executioner, might have scrawled it. Insofar as it was decipherable, a sample passage read:

"Your parents most wronged   himself by saying he had entertained the same idea in John Adams *and* Potomac *but had not ripened into   Do you not think that a mania which should   Certainly."*

Mackenzie was able later to expand these chaotic notes into pages of grisly narrative.

The time element in the Spencer interview is worth consideration. Twice in his report, the commander emphasized that it lasted *"more than an hour."* For more than an hour, Mackenzie perched on a campstool beside the boy and diligently wrote.

If it is true that the fragmentary memorandum represents all that the sailor-author penned during that time, in more than an hour he set down in haste 302 words.

CHAPTER 12

Catharsis

*"The certainty of the guilt of all the three had been placed
beyond peradventure by the ocular view of the commander
and the summary inquest before the council of officers."*
—ALEXANDER SLIDELL MACKENZIE.

THE ANTIPATHIES of violent light and restless shadow,
infinities of sky and bluer sea, belittled the scene that Mackenzie had inserted, for an unstipulated reason that may have
been belated prudence, in the drama he earlier had arranged.
If any of the patiently waiting crew saw indecency in the
hushed conference between the manacled boy on the arms
chest and the glittering officer who, squatting on a campstool,
zealously scribbled, Mackenzie was blind to it. Otherwise, he
could not have reported at such relishful length his efforts to
extort from the young man he intended to hang further excuses
for doing so.

The bell had struck eight. Noon had come and gone. On the
horizon, cloud was rising with blackness in its belly. Mackenzie
continued to write, question Spencer, and write again. The reason why he had suspended the elaborate formality of the execution, the benefit he hoped to gain from the excruciatingly
extended interview, are equally presumptive—yet plausible.

The captain of the *Somers* had begun to hang three men
and then had faltered. His report does not explain this ebbing
of a Spartan purpose, yet it quite well might have been due to

149

his sudden recollection that one of the condemned was no ordinary miscreant but the son of the choleric Secretary of War. Stabbed by that realization, the commander must have felt that his own belief, the verdict of the officers' council, and the opinion of the petty officers were still an insufficient warrant for killing Philip Spencer.

It is entirely likely that Alexander Slidell Mackenzie, the self-admiring author, was more than willing to sacrifice expedition to art and delayed the hangings while he collected all available material for the memorable narrative he intended to write. From any angle, he was not at that moment a heroic or even a reputable figure.

The commander still recoiled from any attempt to wring from the chief conspirator cogent information concerning the extent of the still unrisen mutiny. He did not even ask the names and the number of those involved. Actually, if fantastically, Mackenzie by the evidence of his own report, discussed with Spencer only the ethical and sentimental aspects of his crime. The captain of a vessel, believed to be critically endangered, never asked a single question concerning the scope and substance of the peril.

Pad on knee, pen in hand, and inkwell beside him, the commander opened the interview with appropriately funereal gravity. Presently, as he worked himself into his role of inquisitor-comforter, Mackenzie began to cry. The ubiquitous James W. Wales observed that *"tears were trickling down his cheeks. It appeared to be a very hard duty for him to perform."*

Mackenzie's first question was conventional: Had Mr. Spencer any last words that he would care to have recorded, any final message he wished to send to friends or relatives?

He had none, the boy replied—this and all subsequent utter-

ances are the commander's version of Spencer's statements—
that anyone would wish to receive. The weight of imminent
extinction lay heavily upon the prisoner, making him disap-
pointingly unresponsive. Mackenzie did his best to rouse him.
An affecting farewell was a requisite in all deathbed interviews.
Persuasion at last prevailed, and Spencer dictated what Mackenzie later swore was his victim's sole message:

*"Tell them that I die wishing them every blessing and hap-
piness. I deserve death for this and many other crimes. There
are few crimes that I have not committed. I feel sincerely penitent and my only fear of death is that my repentance may be
too late."*

(NOTE: Mackenzie's chaotic memorandum, written during
the interview, says Spencer confessed that he deserved death
"for this and many other sins." There is a difference. That
same memorandum does not record numerous statements that
the commander later quoted at length and allegedly verbatim.)

This confession was more promising. The boy's repentance,
properly exploited, might lead him into more thorough self-in-
crimination. Had not Mr. Spencer, the commander persisted,
in the commission of his assorted crimes-sins, injured some person? Was not someone suffering unjustly because of Mr. Spencer's misdeeds? If so, there was still time to make reparation.

Mackenzie waited hopefully.

"I have wronged many persons," the boy said at last, *"but
chiefly my parents."* He added out of desolation: *"This will kill
my poor mother."*

"I was not before aware," Mackenzie reported, blind to bio-
logical probabilities, *"that he had a mother."*

The commander admitted that the disclosure for a moment
unmanned him. This reference to motherhood may have been

the emotional cue that set him to weeping. Tearfully, Mackenzie resumed his fishing expedition.

He agreed that Spencer's present situation was distressful, but would it not, he propounded, have been infinitely worse if his wicked plot had succeeded?

"*I do not know what I would have done if it had succeeded,*" the boy granted, and his examiner at once enlightened him.

If the mutiny had prevailed, Cromwell would have killed Spencer, and then McKinley—for reasons obscure, Mackenzie's later nomination for villain-in-chief—"*would have cleared the whole of them from his path.*"

Conversation that seemed to be leading nowhere in particular may have roused in the captive the piteous hope that his life was to be spared. Surely an executioner would not gossip with his victim in a cordial, if tear-sodden, fashion. The son of a lifelong politician said:

"*I fear that this may injure my father.*"

Mackenzie had prompt answer for this, too. Secretary of War Spencer, he proclaimed with opaque logic, would have been injured far more if his son had been taken home for trial. In that event, Philip Spencer never would have received just punishment for his manifold iniquities, since "*for those who have friends or money in America, there is no punishment for the worst of crimes.*"

"*Perhaps,*" the commander temporized in his report, "*this was an extreme or erroneous opinion which I do not attempt to justify. I am only faithfully recording what passed on the occasion.*"

The intimate exchange, the longest and most personal talk he ever had held with his superior, was thawing the prisoner, who now confided:

"*I will tell you frankly what I intended to do, had I got home: I would have attempted to escape. I had the same project aboard the* John Adams *and the* Potomac. *It seemed to be a mania with me.*"

"*Do you not think that this is a mania that should be discouraged in the navy?*"

"*I do, most certainly,*" the about-to-be "*discouraged*" boy replied, "*but have you not formed an exaggerated estimate of the extent of this conspiracy?*"

This was a slight the commander was not inclined to bear. He repelled it by summarizing for Spencer's benefit all the culprit's "*systematic efforts to corrupt the crew and prepare them for the indulgence of every evil passion.*"

The scathing recital must have blighted whatever hope of reprieve had been quickened in the prisoner. The end plainly was near, and time was running out. Spencer tried to delay it. He asked:

"*But are you not going too far? Are you not fast? Does the law entirely justify you?*" and Mackenzie, prosecuting his feline enterprise, bared his claws.

"*I replied that he had not consulted me in making his arrangements; that his opinion could not be an unprejudiced one; that I had consulted all his brother officers, his messmates included, except the boys, and I placed before him their opinion.*"

If the commander had hoped to pull the friendless eighteen-year-old down to his own lachrymose level, he again was frustrated. By his enemy's own admission, the boy kept his composure during the suceeding emotional orgy, which was accompanied by widespread weeping and wild farewell speeches. If, in the last moment of existence, Philip Spencer faltered, that weakness makes the dignity of his earlier conduct still more pathetic.

He could cherish, after Mackenzie's last, spiteful retort, no more delusions concerning his own fate. Spencer only asked with pardonable curiosity what was to be the manner of his death, and begged that he might be shot, instead of hanged. His inquisitor refused to grant his plea.

The commander was pleased, however, to accede to his victim's request that his face might be covered and, finding that the hitherto neglected Cromwell and Small were of the same mind, had a black handkerchief brought from the chief conspirator's locker and two jumpers fetched to blindfold his accomplices. Again, Spencer asked for more time—for a single hour in which to prepare himself.

"No answer was made to this request but he was not hurried and more than the hour he asked for was allowed to elapse."

Mackenzie refused his captive's request that his irons be removed, but when Spencer asked for a Bible and a prayer book, the commander supplied them and had additional copies issued to Cromwell and Small. Thereafter, the executioner-inquisitor assumed with no perceptible strain the additional role of father-confessor. When Spencer blurted out his doubt as to whether so belated a repentance could be acceptable to the deity, Mackenzie *"called to his recollection the case of the penitent thief who was pardoned by our Savior upon the cross."*

The pious citation did not entirely soothe a spirit in death's thickening shadow. While the man who had condemned him waited, still expectantly, Spencer thumbed through the Bible, turned to the prayer book, and finding there what he had sought, slid down from the arms chest with a clash of metal and, weighted as he was, knelt in prayer under the close observance of his resplendent superior.

The boy looked up at last and in travail, common to a time when the dimensions of the Kingdom and the nature of its Ruler were more exactly charted, appealed again to the only visible authority for reassurance.

"*I told him,*" Mackenzie reported, "*that God, who was all-merciful as well as all-wise, could not only understand the difficulties of his situation but extend to him such a measure of mercy as his necessities might require.*"

After administering this comfort, the commander bestowed on the penitent his personal forgiveness, and then turned away to proceed with the hangings.

Spencer torturously hauled himself up on the campstool, and Daniel McKinley remembered how he sat there, bowed, with his head on his shackled hands. The stalled enterprise, which had begun more than an hour before, got itself together and moved forward again. Two petty officers, detailed to drag the boy to the place of execution, for the chain-laden condemned were unable to walk unaided, lifted him from his stool and drew him forward into a morass of lachrymose hysteria.

If the commander reported the excesses of this frenzy incompletely, neither human dignity nor his own reputation suffered from his omissions. It is quite possible that he missed something during this sentimental wallowing, since the disorder was general, but he carefully observed and recorded all the actions and reactions of Alexander Slidell Mackenzie in a time of maudlin extremity.

Weeping began almost at once and spread. Spencer and his conductors came face to face with Cromwell and his escort in the narrow passage between trunk and pump well at the break of the quarter-deck. Neither prisoner appeared to see the other; no word passed between them, but Spencer, turning to Mackenzie, asked if he might speak to Wales.

"When Mr. Wales came up, Mr. Spencer, extending his hand to him, said: 'Mr. Wales, I earnestly hope you will forgive me for tampering with your fidelity.'"

Mackenzie observed that the doomed boy was *"wholly unmoved."* It was his betrayer who choked and began to sob.

"I do forgive you," he blubbered, *"from the bottom of my heart, and I hope that God may forgive you, also."*

"Farewell," Spencer said and turned away.

"Farewell," Wales echoed. He was *"weeping and causing others to weep."*

Spencer had been hauled only a little farther when he met Elisha Small. The little man was in a less tearful and accommodating mood. The impression that he had been cheated outrageously had become fixed in his limited mind. The price he was about to pay for piddling gifts of brandy, tobacco, and cash was hideously exorbitant. He was in the worst of possible plights through his indulgent lip service to a preposterous "conspiracy," and he glared at its instigator when Spencer begged:

"Small, forgive me for getting you into this trouble."

"Forgive you!" the little man snarled. *"No, by God, Mr. Spencer, I can't forgive you."*

The boy repeated his plea. Small shook his head stubbornly and babbled:

"Ah, Mr. Spencer, that is a hard thing for you to ask me. We shall soon be before the face of God, and then we shall know all about it."

"You must forgive me, Small," Spencer begged. *"I cannot die without your forgiveness."*

Mackenzie, thus far only a bystander, now proceeded to take the play away from his subordinates. He intervened and persuaded Small to pardon his seducer. The commander then displayed his own magnanimity. He grasped Small's hand and forgave him. Mr. Wales saw, through his own tears, that both men were crying.

The moist protestations of executioner and about-to-be-executed were extensive. Mackenzie must have esteemed them greatly since he reported them at length. The spiritual kinsman of Captain Reece, commanding H.M.S. *Mantelpiece,* inquired if he had done anything that demanded Small's pardon. If so, he would willingly beg for it.

"I asked him what I had ever said or done to him to make him seek my life, conscious of no injustice or provocation of any sort. I felt that it was yet necessary to my comfort to receive the assurance from his own lips. If any wrong had been done him—if any word of harshness in the impatience or excitement of duty had escaped me, I was ready myself to ask also for forgiveness."

The little seaman's impressionable mind was fired by this display of nobility, and he tried to surpass it. After all, Elisha Small rated the leading part in the dialogue. It was he who was going to be hanged.

"What have you done to me, Captain Mackenzie?" he cried, momentarily checking the other's eloquence. *"What have you done to me, sir? Nothing, but treat me like a man."*

He might briefly halt but he could not hush the commander.

"I told him in justification of the course which I was pursuing that I had high responsibilities to fulfil; that there were duties that I owed to the government which had entrusted me with this vessel, to the officers under my command. . . . There was yet a higher duty to [He never missed!] *the flag of my country."*

Small snatched up this cue and got in a few words edgewise.

"You are right, sir," he choked. *"You are doing your duty and I honor you for it. God bless that flag and prosper it."*

He wheeled about to face the line of men, holding the whip reserved for him.

"Now, brother topmates," he cried. *"Give me a quick and easy death."*

Small suffered himself to be half led, half dragged in his irons to the noose assigned him. A jumper was pulled down over his face. The paralyzed muster at last was purposefully and obediently in motion. The fifer and drummer reported to Mackenzie. Spencer was placed abaft Small. To starboard, the loop at the whip's end was being settled about Cromwell's bull neck. The dark cloud was piling up in the far distance, and the wind blew coolly.

Gansevoort turned away, after adjusting the black handkerchief over Spencer's face. The boy called to him:

"You may judge for yourself whether I die like a coward or a brave man," and, striving to fend off terror by brittle hardihood, asked the privilege of giving the command for his own death.

Mr. Gansevoort, at the moment, was too shaken to estimate anyone's bravery, for he, himself, had recently suffered another severe fright. His peculiar gift for forming judgments from personal appearances had made him believe that he had barely escaped murder at Cromwell's hands while bidding him farewell.

"He grasped my arm very firmly and held it tight. He asked me to forgive him and bade me good-bye; said that he was innocent and hoped that before six months we would find it out. I turned my arm to get clear of his grasp but he held onto me.

"In a few minutes, he relaxed his hold and struck his hands

clear. I had an idea that he meant to take me overboard with him."

That idea still was upsetting the lieutenant when he carried Spencer's request to Mackenzie.

The commander, again letting his purpose go slack, crossed the deck to where the noosed and blindfolded boy waited. Spencer, incurably romantic, wanted to know exactly how his life was to be ended. Mackenzie obligingly told him.

The execution was to be conducted with all possible formality. When fife and drum sounded the call for hoisting the colors, the national ensign would be run up to the peak. The drummer would then beat three rolls, and during the last of these a gun would be fired. The explosion would be a signal for the actual hanging.

Spencer asked through the masking handkerchief if the schedule might be altered. He wished, in fulfillment of his boast to Gansevoort, to give the order for the gun's discharge. Mackenzie granted the request and dismissed the drummer and fifer. The boy then asked a final favor. He begged, already familiar with the torments of delay, that there be no interval between his word of command and the carronade's discharge. He girded himself to order his own execution, but there was a further, excruciating pause.

Small, having overheard the conversation, demanded an equivalent privilege. He wished to deliver a farewell address. The commander inquired if Mr. Spencer was willing to wait, and when the boy consented, ordered the impromptu hood pulled back from the face of the little seaman, who seems to have been Mackenzie's favorite victim. Small shouted frantically:

"*Shipmates and topmates, take warning by my example. I never was a pirate; I never killed a man. It's for saying I would do it that I am about to depart this life. See what a word will do. It was going in a Guineaman that brought me to this. Beware of a Guineaman."*

His breath ran out. When he regained it, he demanded with a vestige of the earlier vindictiveness:

"I am now ready to die, Mr. Spencer. Are you?"

Cromwell, hitherto ignored in Mackenzie's pageant, groaned through his muffling jumper:

"Tell my wife I die an innocent man. Tell Lieutenant Morris"—a person no further identified—*"I die an innocent man."*

The commander duly recorded his principal detestation's last words and immediately besmirched them.

"But it had been the game of this man to appear innocent, to urge Mr. Spencer on, to furnish him with professional ideas, to bring about a catastrophe, of which Mr. Spencer was to take all the risk and from which he, Cromwell, was to derive all the benefit.

"He had taken a great many precautions to appear innocent," the commander reported, *"but he had not taken enough."*

The torment at last was ending. There could be no further excuse for delay. Mackenzie clambered onto the trunk where his *"eye could take in everything."* His uniform flashed. The sibilant sounds of wind and water, the stir and harsh breathing of expectant men, filled the increasingly taut wait for Spencer's self-extinguishing command.

The boy stood blindfolded and silent. He wavered and mumbled something that only Oliver Browning, acting boatswain, caught. He reported hastily to Mackenzie that Mr. Spencer found himself unable to give the word.

"Stand by," Mackenzie shouted at once. *"Fire."*

The carronade roared and recoiled. Through scudding smoke, Gansevoort cried: "*Whips!*"

Feet scuffled, found purchase, and tramped as the men walked away with the lines. Three heavily burdened figures suddenly were buoyant. They shot aloft, whirling with a clear clinking of their irons, swooping in ever briefer arcs as their tethers ran in through the blocks. Below the yardarm, the bodies of Spencer, Cromwell, and Small halted. They spun and balanced, triple blacknesses against the glaring sky, until at last conforming to the brig's motion, they swung in unison to and fro.

Behind the swaying bodies, the wind spread the flag's bright fabric, and Alexander Slidell Mackenzie, beholding his work and finding it good, felt another speech coming on. The crew were ordered to gather about the trunk, and from this pulpit their captain preached to them while the restless dead above him pointed the morals of his sermon.

Mackenzie, for the benefit of Secretary Upshur and possibly a larger audience, reported his singular address almost verbatim. The orator, with grisly courtesy, saluted the man and woman whom he had bereaved, particularly Spencer's "*distinguished father whose talents and character had raised him to one of the highest stations in the land.*"

No such exalted and exalting qualities had distinguished John Canfield Spencer's late son.

"*After a few months service at sea most wretchedly spent, so far as the acquisition of professional knowledge was concerned, he had aspired to replace me in command which I had only reached after thirty years of faithful servitude.*"

With the example of righteous diligence on the trunk and the bodies of the iniquitous reeling overhead, Mackenzie besought his crew to be zealous and temperate and to let their lives be guided *"by truth, honor and fidelity."* They should beware of Cromwell's greed for gold. In that connection, Boatswain's Mate William Collins had a tale that his captain would like him to tell the crew.

Collins, called forward, stumbled through his story of service aboard an Indiaman. Her supercargo, *"a Mr. Thorndyke"* had a keg of doubloons aboard. Collins knew where it was hidden but he told no man of its presence. Cromwell, hearing the story, had laughed at its narrator and had said if he had been in Collins' place he would have run off with the keg.

"I told the boys," Mackenzie informed Upshur, *"that they had only to choose between the morality of Cromwell and that of Collins—Cromwell at the yardarm and Collins, piping his call."*

Small, too, had been brought to his death by avarice and an addiction to brandy.

"He had, however, at least died invoking blessings on [inevitably!] *the flag of his country."*

Mackenzie stepped from the trunk, and the crew was dismissed. As they trooped forward, the commander was pained to see that some apprentices looked aloft and giggled. The bodies at the yardarm—Cromwell's toward its starboard end, Small's near its center, and Spencer's to larboard—still kept time to the vessel's motion, with masked heads bowed as though in solemn thought, with necks craned by the weight of their irons.

The discontent that is an occupational disease of all artists was depressing Mackenzie. He had done his best to adorn a climactic moment, yet he felt that his performance, however creditable, had not been all he had hoped. His audience was dispersing. Something should be done to lift the scene higher, to end it on a more stirring note.

The commander ordered the crew mustered aft again and, seizing an ever reliable expedient, submitted it to the ever reliable Gansevoort.

"The commander asked me how it would do to give three cheers. I told him I thought it would do well. When the men came aft, he said: 'My lads, three cheers to the American flag.'"

The response abolished Mackenzie's distress.

"Never were three heartier cheers given. In that electric moment, I did not doubt that the patriotism of even the worst of the conspirators for an instant broke forth. I felt that I once more was completely commander of the vessel that was entrusted to me, equal to whatever the honor of my country might require."

The crew was piped down to its long-postponed dinner. There remained on deck only the men required to work the brig. Above them, three bodies continued to swing to the *Somers'* rolling. When the crew had dined, the commander ordered the dead men lowered. The swelling cloud now blackened half the sky.

Mackenzie, the part-time literary man, reported with necrophile zest the disposal of the men he had hanged. The funeral of Spencer, Cromwell and Small was even more dilatory than their execution, but nothing connected with the ceremony or its preliminaries escaped the avid eye and eloquent pen of the *Somers'* captain.

The closest associates of the dead were ordered to remove their chains and prepare them for burial. Messmates received the bodies of Cromwell and Small, and the midshipmen,

Spencer's. Mackenzie records his earnest wish that the boy's body, as befitted an officer's, be coffined. The commander was willing to tear up part of the berth deck to obtain the needful lumber, but the always helpful Mr. Gansevoort offered two empty mess chests, and these were made to serve.

When preparations were completed, the lieutenant invited Mackenzie to inspect the result, and the commander, in general, was pleased. Spencer, in uniform but without his sword, *"which he had forfeited the right to wear,"* had been placed in his mess-chest-coffin on the starboard side of the quarterdeck. Forward, Cromwell and beyond him, Small, lay on the hammocks that would be stitched about them.

Mackenzie *"noticed with pain that the taste of one of the sailors had led him to bind the hands of Cromwell with a riband, having on it in gold letters the name of that chivalrous Somers who had died a self-devoted victim to the cause of his country."*

The commander, despite his anguish, let the ribbon remain since it had been *"dishonored by the treason of its wearer."* He had become interested in a scar that ran up from Cromwell's forehead, into his hair. Mackenzie ordered the funeral postponed while his erstwhile boatswain's head was shaved.

The *Somers'* captain found that the delay had been worth while for the dead man's bared skull was crisscrossed by scars. Mackenzie was satisfied that these proved that his victim *"had been where wounds had been given and received."* He then gave the disfigured body a final, verbal kick.

"Cromwell, by his own admission had been a slaver and had been an inmate of the Moro Castle at Havana. It was the general impression of the honest part of the crew that he already had been a pirate."

The brig's company had been so engrossed in this ghoulish

investigation that the squall, coming down after ample warning, caught the Somers unprepared. The blast fifed in her
rigging, drummed on her sails. Men, skittering across the
suddenly canted deck, could do no more in the moment of
danger than cast tarpaulins over the dead to shield them from
the sluicing rain.

It was dusk before the brief tempest passed. It was night
when Spencer, Cromwell, and Small at last were buried. The
protean commander—judge, executioner, reporter, and now
minister—read the committal service by the light of the battle
lanterns. These and lesser lamps, held by members of the
crew, filled the space immediately about the hammock-swathed
figures and the makeshift coffin with ruddy brilliance. Beyond
the glowing area, hung the blackness of sky and sea.

Men and boys crammed the gangway and flowed up over
the booms where, six nights earlier, Philip Spencer had sat
with James W. Wales and had asked him hollowly:

"Whales, do you fear to die?"

The responses to the service, Mackenzie noted, were
"audibly and devoutly made."

He spoke the last words of the committal. Hammock sails
lowered the bodies overside. Darkness took them. There were
three faint splashes. The commander lifted his voice in prayer.
He besought the Almighty that he and his crew might "return
in safety to enjoy the blessings of the land with the fruit of
our labor and with thankful remembrance of Thy mercies."

Voices chorused, "Amen." Mackenzie closed his prayer
book.

"I could not but humbly hope that divine sanction would
not be wanting to the deed of that day."

The captain of the Somers, in the weeks succeeding his

pious aspiration, must have believed ever more firmly that the deity had approved of his conduct, had even inspired and directed him. All the omens were auspicious.

The monstrous terror that had pervaded the brig, whatever its source and substance, had been appeased by a triple immolation. Mackenzie had been restored to complete command of his vessel and himself. Each uneventful day of the homeward voyage confirmed that reinstatement. Healing calm had followed the tempest, and when the wind revived, it blew fair.

After the brig that he had wrested from the clutching hands of mutineers had returned to New York with eleven prisoners to exemplify perils endured and victory won; after pulpit, press, and populace had applauded the Roman conduct of her captain, Alexander Slidell Mackenzie must have become even more confident of divine approbation. It had set him in a lofty place; it had filled his ears with the sweet sound of praise; it had moved him to strive for still greater elegance as he wrote the final pages of the expanded report he shortly would forward to the Secretary of the Navy.

Bent over a desk in his brother-in-law's navy yard dwelling, with the glow of creation warming him, the captain of the *Somers* was not aware immediately that the lately favoring wind was backing around into the east and had begun to blow more coldly.

CHAPTER 13

Rising Wind

"The mental obliquity, so very obvious throughout the whole affair, renders any ordinary analysis of human motives exceedingly precarious."—JAMES FENIMORE COOPER.

THE CLOUD, at its beginning, was no larger than a man's hand and easy to overlook in the sky's continued brilliance. Alexander Slidell Mackenzie, raptly contemplating his own new fame, was not immediately conscious of the small intruding shadow. Approval of his courageous deed was on every tongue and was amplified in every New York paper. Untempered admiration for the commander who, when faced with a grim duty, had feared neither man, devil, nor the Secretary of War, was rippling out from New York across the young republic. Condemnation of the precocious young monster the *Somers'* captain had slain was equally unqualified.

No better sounding board for celebration or defamation could have been found than the gawky and blatant adolescent city of 300,000 souls crammed into the toe of Manhattan Island. It lately had been a provincial town; it was now becoming a metropolis.

New York was then, and thenceforth, a city of contrasts, material and emotional. In 1842, it was a place of pompous elegance and appalling slums, of many churches and more brothels. Its lardy aristocracy was stubbornly conservative; its

167

advanced thinkers were babbling of dress reforms, votes for women, free love, and the millennial gospel according to Fourier; its polyglot proletariat was addicted to rioting.

It was a vociferous, brawling, sensation-loving young city, hungry for news that, in general, came to it stale. Still-fragmentary railroads were expediting the arrival of intelligence, and in another two years Professor Morse's invention, the telegraph, would further accelerate delivery. In 1842, Philadelphia was six hours distant, and Washington twelve. Tidings from Europe took weeks to reach Manhattan, and news from China, then embroiled with Britain in the Opium War, was frequently six months late.

The story of the *Somers'* mutiny, delivered piping hot on Manhattan's doorstep, aroused and enraptured a volatile citizenry.

New York was then a sea-nourished town, with water-front streets raftered by the bowsprits of ships from all the quarters of the globe; a town whose enterprises still were more closely linked to the tides than to landsmen's clocks; a town, vitally dependent upon ocean-borne commerce, with advertisements of packets about to sail to ports of the seven seas cramming the back pages of the newspapers.

"Piracy" and "mutiny" were not luridly romantic words to New Yorkers of the 1840's. They offered actual menace to the city's welfare. The tale of Spencer's conspiracy was, to thousands of residents, the story of a peril to their livelihood that had been valiantly destroyed. Alexander Slidell Mackenzie deserved well of his fellow citizens.

They said so, full-throatedly, and the press enlarged and formalized their approval. The newspapers of the truculent, strident town reflected their readers' propensity for quarreling. Editors, however much denunciation they spent upon public questions and the politically unclean, usually had a large additional store to exercise against each other but, in this instance, their praise of the captain of the *Somers* was phenomenally unanimous.

Mackenzie, editorials proclaimed, by his stern courage, by his sublime refusal to discriminate between the highborn conspirator and the low, by his display of all the Roman virtues, constantly extolled and seldom practiced in the youthful nation, had averted untold calamity and had added new luster to the United States Navy.

"*Thus,*" Horace Greeley exulted, "*by the prompt and fearless decision of Captain Mackenzie, one of the most bold and daring conspiracies ever formed was frustrated and crushed.*"

He went on, crescendo, with even less than his usual regard for English usage:

"*The* Somers *is the swiftest vessel in the service, was fully manned and equipped and capable of the greatest efficacy in any belligerent cause.*

"*Suppose this vessel had been converted into a Pirate Ship, sailing under the black flag which denounces war and death to the whole world, under the command of as desperate and determined a ruffian as Spencer and acting in conjunction with confederates of similar character.*

"*Who can tell how many of our packet ships would have fallen victim to his prowess—how many hundreds of worthy men would have been murdered in cold blood—how many women would have been devoted to a fate infinitely more horrible than the most cruel death that the hellish ingenuity of devils could devise? What inconceivable horrors would have made the thought of an ocean voyage dread and terror to the heart of the world. . . .*

"We see not how it is possible in this view of the case for a single instant to entertain other feelings than that of unqualified admiration and profound gratitude for the decision and firmness with which they were prevented."

Philip Spencer, according to the *Tribune* was a precociously evil being, twenty years old, who had been shipped home from the Brazil Squadron for an unspecified, and inferentially unprintable, offense. To avoid punishment he had promised to leave the navy after he had been returned to New York but, arriving there, had broken his pledge.

For once, Horace Greeley found himself in agreement with his fellow editors. Rival newspapers followed his lead or tried to outstrip him in maligning the dead and extolling their executioner.

In the massed journalistic baying, it is doubtful whether New Yorkers noticed the *Tribune*'s favorable review of Thomas Babington Macaulay's new book of ballads, *The Lays of Ancient Rome*, or paid much attention to its report of the large sales recorded by Samuel Lover's *Handy Andy*. The *Somers* tragedy overshadowed the debut of General Tom Thumb at P. T. Barnum's American Museum and weakened interest in the rival headliner at the National Museum—Mr. Nellis, *"born without arms"* who nevertheless was *"performing on many musical instruments and willing to shave anyone in the audience."*

Echoes of popular acclaim penetrated even the seclusion of the commandant's residence in the Brooklyn Navy Yard and inspired Mackenzie, still assiduously at work upon his second report, to bestow a higher literary gloss upon its final pages. James Fenimore Cooper later styled this composition with some accuracy:

"The most extraordinary document of this sort, perhaps, that ever was laid before the world."

Mr. Cooper was one of a few tough-minded people who, from the outset, refused to be dazzled by the splendor of the commander's deed. The author of the Leatherstocking novels, a truculent person with a low boiling point, had no lawsuits in progress at the moment to divert his mind from the *Somers* affair. He immediately denounced Mackenzie vocally and vehemently. Later he was to assail him in print. The pamphlet Cooper published played its part in evoking the tempest. By now, the wind was imperceptibly shifting and beginning to blow.

Gansevoort had delivered his captain's first dispatch to the Secretary of the Navy. John Canfield Spencer had learned from Mr. Upshur how and why his son had been hanged. Through the clamorous praise of Alexander Slidell Mackenzie and the reckless defamation of Philip Spencer, there suddenly rose a solitary, never surely identified voice, speaking publicly in defense of the boy and of the humbler men who had died with him.

On December 21, the *Tribune* published a letter it had lifted from the *Washington Madisonian* of the nineteenth. The writer's familiarity with Mackenzie's first dispatch, his evident knowledge of Philip Spencer and his career, and the signature "S" at the letter's end all indicate that the Secretary of War was its author, though later John Canfield Spencer officially denied it.

There was no trace of the father's notorious temper in this first open defense of his son. The writer of the letter charged at its outset that the information upon which the New York newspapers had based their extravagant stories had been *"fur-*

nished by some of the officers who had had a hand in the bloody deed."

The communication pursued, more calmly than a choleric and lately bereaved parent might be expected to write:

"This is evident from its containing some facts that could be known only to those officers—but these were so perverted, so exaggerated and interspersed with so much surmise and so much downright falsehood as to evince the deep anxiety felt to make sure of the first impression on the public mind.

"An awful responsibility rests upon these officers and, above all, on their commander. Without the least desire to make that responsibility more hazardous than now it is, it is still deemed an act of simple and bare justice to the memory of the slain to say that the examination of the papers transmitted by Commander Mackenzie shows these facts. . . ."

The anonymous author then pointed out what other legalists later stressed: by Mackenzie's own report, there had been no mutinous disorder aboard the *Somers* during the four days that had elapsed between the arrest of the alleged ringleaders and their execution. Furthermore, "S" maintained, the officers' court that condemned Spencer, Small, and Cromwell to death was scandalously incompetent and wholly indifferent to elemental principles of law.

None of the accused were permitted to testify, or to cross-examine the witnesses against him, or to face these accusers.

"The officers were without even the form of a court; without even the obligation of an oath and, upon this ex-parte secret information, they united in the opinion that the safety of the ship required that the prisoners be put to death. How far this recommendation was influenced by the acts or fears of Mackenzie does not appear."

These were bold words, thrust against the current of popular enthusiasm. The flood was not halted, but sober men, reading this first defense of the hitherto unbefriended dead, were troubled by its authentic ring and wondered whether the captain of the *Somers* was entirely the hero the press and public had proclaimed him. Might he not, in his role of a seagoing Lucius Junius Brutus, have overplayed his part?

The letter's author dinned again on the fact that *"the men were hanged when everything and person were perfectly quiet after four days of perfect security."* Thereafter, he spoke, still calmly, in defense of the forlorn Philip Spencer and the men who had died with him.

Anent the late acting midshipman's dark past, which Mr. Greeley and others had zestfully publicized, it was not true that Spencer had promised to resign from the navy and then had gone back on his word. He had resigned on his return to New York from service with the Brazil Squadron, but:

"He had been restored to his rank, without influence by his friends, by the Secretary of the Navy on the recommendation of his commanding officer [because of] the nature and circumstances of his offense—inebriation."

There had been additional inaccuracy in the charges brought against the boy. Philip had not been more than twenty years old. *"If he had lived to January 28th, he would have been nineteen."*

Finally "S" asked for justice, urging that it be not withheld *"because one of the victims was connected with a high functionary of the government, nor because another was unknown and had not a friend nor a relation on the face of the earth."*

That citation most nearly applied to Small. Cromwell had a recently wedded wife, and Margaret E. Cromwell, possibly in association with John Canfield Spencer, already had retained a lawyer for the purpose of dragging the slayer of her husband out from under the navy's wing and into court.

The commander remained upon his new pedestal, yet the anonymous attack had perceptibly rocked it, and another incident occurred that was to diminish his heroic stature and increasingly trouble him.

He had devoted the final pages of his second and fuller report to praise of his conspicuously loyal subordinates and had recommended promotion for a number of them. Indiscreetly, he had gone further.

There was a purblindness, a callousness, in the commander that, even when he was most acute, kept him singularly unresponsive to the requirements of propriety or elemental decency, and doubtless popular adulation had made him more indifferent. Mackenzie saw nothing unseemly in proposing that his nephew be awarded the berth of the boy the uncle lately had hanged.

It was not a tactful request, and the messenger he chose for its delivery made the suggestion more indelicate still. Piling one stupidity upon another, the captain of the *Somers* detailed young Oliver H. Perry to carry the newly completed second report to Washington, thereby thrusting both nephew and uncle into more serious trouble than the letter signed by "S" had caused them.

The youthful Perry constitutionally talked too much and knew too little. It flattered him to be questioned by a greatly concerned Secretary of the Navy, who doubtless, if he acquitted himself well, would promote him into the place of the late Philip Spencer. Perry babbled to Upshur a scandalous and never-to-be-verified tale.

Hadn't Philip Spencer left any last message to ease his

parents' bereavement, no letter, no written word whatever? the secretary asked, with the grim grief of his colleague in mind.

Oh, indeed he had, Perry replied eagerly. Spencer had dictated a letter to the commander himself. The nephew had seen him do it.

There had been no mention of any such letter in either of Mackenzie's reports. Neither the Spencer father nor mother had received any word whatever from their dead son. If Philip had dictated a message, where was it?

Well, Perry did not exactly know. He remained certain that a letter had been taken down by his uncle, just before young Spencer's death.

Oliver H. Perry returned from Washington without the hoped-for midshipman's warrant. He was greeted intemperately by his late sponsor for promotion, whose shining fame the young man had done his garrulous best to blight. Mackenzie succeeded in convincing Upshur that no such farewell letter had ever existed, and evidence available today seems to support the assertion, but the tale got loose and caused the commander great damage.

The story, whispered in Washington, later was shouted in New York by Spencer's suddenly vocal defenders. Men who had recently hailed Mackenzie as a hero switched about and debated whether he were not the world's blackest villain. "Constant Reader" and "Pro Bono Publico" wrote defaming letters to the papers. Literary friends of the commander came to his rescue incautiously with countercommunications, defaming the defamers, and politics, which in that vivacious time seldom could be kept out of any human activity for long, invaded and further confused the *Somers* affair.

The harmonious editorial praises, so gratifying to the commander, relapsed into dissonance. The partisan press of the 1840's customarily grasped any issue that could be used as a club to belabor the opposition. It was not difficult to turn the conduct of Alexander Slidell Mackenzie into such a weapon.

Since the Secretary of War, whose son had been hanged, was a proved traitor to the true faith and had flaunted his perfidy by joining the cabinet of the archheretic, Tyler, Whig newspapers continued to defend the commander. The pro-administration press, deftly swallowing its late approval, denounced him. Editors went to work, for or against Mackenzie, with even less restraint than that usually imposed by journalistic ethics, which had no strictures against gouging, kneeing, or biting. The ensuing vituperation professedly shocked one who was no mean vituperator himself. James Fenimore Cooper wrote:

"The journals that had blindly plunged into the subject found no difficulty in maintaining their first opinions, under every state of the facts. Their object was to support one side of the question, let the truth lie where it might. The moving causes were political animosity, mercantile cupidity and personal interests . . . demoniacal passions having been exhibited in a nakedness of deformity that is unusual even in our own greatly degraded press."

The wind was getting up. Alexander Slidell Mackenzie, lately and unanimously acclaimed, began to look nervously about him for shelter.

Christmas stood on the doorstep, and the tempo of yuletide revelry was quickening. On the evening of December 22, George Bancroft lectured to an enraptured citizenry on "The Battle of Bunker Hill," while Richard A. Dana held another full house spellbound with an address entitled "A Search for the Sources of Noble Action."

Gelatine turkeys and pickled oysters were featured delicacies for the holiday season, and the *Morning Courier and Enquirer* was campaigning against the atrociously high cost of meat due, it was charged, to a conspiracy among the market men. Mutton, the outraged journal revealed, had rocketed to six cents a pound; chicken, to seven or eight; prime beef, to ten; and turkeys, to a ruinous twelve cents per pound.

In a closed and appropriately darkened Washington house the Secretary of War, the man of few friends, had shut himself up with his grief and his bitter plans for vengeance. None of the growing yuletide cheer entered the hushed dwelling, and only one intimate passed through a briefly opened doorway. On Christmas Eve, John Lorimer Graham, New York's postmaster, wrote to Silas M. Stilwell, United States marshal in New York:

"Our friend Spencer is stricken down. He wishes impartial but stern justice done in this matter. It is a case that will agitate the nation and the facts will disclose a case unparalleled in the history of civilized nations. . . . Mr. S. has seen no one outside his family but myself. I spent two hours with him today."

John Canfield Spencer had read Mackenzie's first dispatch to Upshur and the second more fulsome report. He must have learned of the callow Oliver Perry's babbling and have believed its every word. The knowledge that he and his son had been in perpetual opposition whetted the father's cold intention. He could mourn Philip most fittingly by exacting from the boy's slayer the utmost in Mosaic retribution.

The Secretary of War determined to get his son's murderer into court—a civilian court, not a naval tribunal. The latter would be manned by brother officers who would be intent primarily on protecting Mackenzie and only secondarily on seeing justice done.

The elder Spencer wanted the sanctimonious hangman brought before a body where his uniform and his colleagues could not shield him. He wanted to see the captain of the *Somers* twist and sweat under examination, as Philip must have sweated for the hour before his death. He longed to watch Mackenzie's face when a jury that could not possibly do otherwise brought in its verdict of guilty. If that was hard, if that was unmerciful, it was infinitely greater mercy than Alexander Slidell Mackenzie had granted John Canfield Spencer's son.

There was the widow Cromwell, too—an admirably determined woman. She, like the Secretary of War, was intent on retribution. It would be well if he and she worked together. It might even be best if, with aid from him, the woman led the attack upon Mackenzie. The nonsense he had advanced for hanging Philip might confuse a jury. The captain of the *Somers* had had no excuse for executing Cromwell but had murdered him out of hand.

Word of Spencer's intention may have reached the increasingly assailed commander. Upshur must have known of it, and Upshur's brother was Mackenzie's close friend. In any event, editorial and popular clamor made it clear that the storm was mounting. For the sake of his reputation and his own personal safety, the captain of the *Somers* dived for the nearest available shelter. He requested that a court of inquiry weigh the propriety of his conduct. The Secretary of the Navy was pleased to grant the appeal and ordered the court to begin its hearings aboard the *North Carolina* in the Brooklyn Navy Yard, December 28.

On December 29, Graham wrote again to Stilwell:

"Mr. S. has returned to his office and yesterday resumed his seat at a cabinet meeting, which is said to have been an affecting meeting. He is looking forward to getting Mackenzie into a civil court."

The commander, though certainly aware by now that Spencer and his associates intended to hunt him down, had a pleasant sense of security while the court of inquiry moved forward a little each day. It was agreeable to sit in his dress uniform and feel that all eyes were upon him. The men who heard his case were his fellow officers—comprehending men, sympathetic men, who understood the ethics and necessities of command.

Gradually, however, as the court droned its way toward a still-distant conclusion, the captain of the *Somers* began to be uneasy again. His reputation was not receiving the expected repairs. Instead, though indirectly, it was being damaged further.

The newspaper accounts of each day's proceedings were forming a picture that bore slight resemblance to the original popular impression of the commander and his heroic deed. Men were beginning to ask each other whether, just possibly, the letter "S" had written might not have been a more accurate statement of the case than Mackenzie's own report.

The *Courier and Enquirer,* property of Mackenzie's friend and neighbor, continued to support him stoutly, but other journals were increasingly hostile. The *Herald,* which at the outset of the inquiry had urged its readers to keep open minds, ignored its own counsel on January 8.

"The newspapers [the editor, James Gordon Bennett, wrote] *are coming out very rapidly against the conduct of Commander Mackenzie and there is hardly a paper that has spoken*

of it that does not consider the execution a high-handed and unnecessary measure. The execution of Cromwell appears to be entirely without cause, without evidence and without necessity. People begin to think it is time for the grand jury to intervene."

This about-face and other straws in the rising wind were forgotten by the commander when suddenly he found himself facing graver, more immediate danger.

On January 12, James B. Scoles, attorney for Margaret E. Cromwell, appeared before Judge Samuel Rossiter Betts of the Federal District Court and applied for a warrant charging Alexander Slidell Mackenzie and Guert Gansevoort with "wilful murder on the high seas."

This Betts refused to issue, holding that the court of inquiry had prior jurisdiction. He had averted the sudden peril; he had not abolished it. The inquiry could not go on forever, and when it had adjourned, Mackenzie would again be vulnerable to civilian prosecution.

In Washington the scandal and Spencer's implacable intention together were thrusting Secretary Upshur and the navy's high brass toward unwelcome decision. Whatever the findings of the tribunal now in session, it was becoming painfully clear that Mackenzie must face trial for his life.

Already he had done disastrous things to the navy's popularity. He had roused too much talk of "quarter-deck tyranny" and "despots in uniform." Something more radical would have to be done, when the court of inquiry had concluded. That was made still more evident on January 20, when Mr. Bennett, who earlier had urged his readers to maintain balanced minds, exploded all over the *Herald*'s editorial page:

"Captain Mackenzie and his officers acted at the time under

*a species of insanity, produced by panic, lively imagination and
the spirit of the age, all working together.*

"Read over carefully his hurried narrative and who will
doubt his perfect insanity? His horrid execution of three men;
his piping down to dinner while these three human bodies
were dangling from the yardarm; the awful dinner talk, full
of horrors, laughter and blood . . . the commendation of his
nephew to fill the shoes of the young man just executed, form
together one of the most awful examples of human intellect
run mad, of human imagination in a state of insanity that the
world ever saw."

In the increasingly notorious case of Alexander Slidell Mackenzie, naval authority, however considerate of its own, would
have to choose between bad and worse: a court-martial for
the commander, or else his surrender to the civil law that the
intransigent John Canfield Spencer was holding in leash until
the court of inquiry ended.

The brass decided it would be best for all concerned, especially Mackenzie, if he were to face trial inside, not outside,
the service. By some unrecorded, monumental feat of persuasion, the Secretary of the Navy convinced the Secretary of War
that this was a sound idea. How Upshur accomplished it, no
one now can tell. Possibly he assured Spencer that the commander would be punished to the full extent of navy law. In
any event he won his contention, for the lately bereaved father
soon afterward had Mackenzie in his hands and let him go.

On January 21, the court of inquiry found Alexander Slidell
Mackenzie guiltless and announced that it could discern no
cause for further action against him. For four days thereafter
the commander was vulnerable to civilian prosecution, yet
neither the recently vengeful elder Spencer nor his associate,
Margaret Cromwell, made a move against him.

On January 25, Upshur, ignoring the court of inquiry's recommendation, wrote thus to Mackenzie:

"*Sir: I transmit a copy of charges and specifications preferred against you by this Department.*

"*A Naval General Court Martial will convene at New York aboard the U. S. N. Carolina on the 1st of Feb'y next, to the presiding officer of which you will report yourself for trial. You will hand to the Judge Advocate a list of your witnesses.*

"*On receipt of this order you will consider yourself under arrest.*"

CHAPTER 14

Ablution

"A *mutiny detected is a mutiny suppressed.*"—JAMES FENI-
MORE COOPER.

THE NAVY'S first protective maneuver had been clumsy and
popularly infuriating. The service had tried to better a bad
situation and had simply made it worse. At the beginning of
the court of inquiry's proceedings, naval authorities had hoped
that further scandal could be averted. By the time the tribunal
reached decision, officials had discovered they couldn't have
been more mistaken.

The top brass would have been willing to accept the court's
findings and forget the whole unfortunate mess as rapidly as
possible. The president of the inquiry, Captain Charles Stewart, and his associates, Commodore A. J. Dallas and Commodore Jacob Jones, by their unanimous opinion had washed
Alexander Slidell Mackenzie as clean as they could get him.
Authority was eager to set him in some secluded spot to dry.

There weren't any secluded spots. Public uproar had invaded them all, and, for the moment at least, the captain of
the *Somers* was being hailed not as a Spartan hero but as the
veritable reincarnation of Cain.

The electorate, roused by editorials like James Gordon Bennett's denunciation and passionately believing, with some
validity, that the court of inquiry had blindly and blandly

ignored the evidence, was screeching still more shrilly for the life of the executioner of Spencer, Cromwell, and Small. Primarily the welfare of the navy was dependent upon the will of the electorate. Its indignation could not be entirely ignored.

Moreover, John Canfield Spencer, though cajoled and half restrained by his fellow Secretary's persuasions, was girding himself for action. Mackenzie each day ran a greater risk of being jailed for murder. He was dropping away like a rocket stick from the brief apogee of his fame. The best the navy could do for its currently execrated officer was to order a court-martial to cushion his fall.

The commander would enjoy a security, he would receive a consideration while standing trial by his colleagues, that he could not expect if he were haled into a civilian court. Perhaps he might gain other still problematical advantages. Courts-martial were stuffy, ponderous, tiresomely deliberate. Who could tell? Before Mackenzie's ended, popular wrath might cool; the whimsical public might become tired of the whole affair, though the noise it was now making was not indicative of any imminent weariness.

The tumult troubled Abel P. Upshur so greatly that on the eve of the court-martial, he wrote a nervous letter to Commodore Jacob Jones, port admiral at New York:

"*Sir: The incidents aboard the* Somers *have attracted so much of public attention & interest and the excitement in the public mind seems to be so intense that I feel a particular anxiety to guard the proceedings of the approaching court Martial, not only from the reality but the* appearance *of partiality or injustice. With this view, I consider it of the utmost importance that the crew of the* Somers *should be so kept as*

*to prevent the possibility of any improper tampering with
them.*

*"What is the best course to be pursued it is impossible for
me to say. I must submit that matter to you & I do so with
entire confidence, desiring only to impress on your mind the
deep conviction of my own that too much caution cannot be
used to ensure the exact truth in the testimony which the
crew may be called upon to give."*

Thus, in one short, deft communication, the Secretary of
the Navy washed his hands, neatly passed the buck, and put
himself in the clear, no matter what happened thereafter. His
admonishing letter may have been wholly sincere yet, if he
truly meant what he wrote, it is odd that Commodore Jones
and his subordinates should so openly have ignored their superior's order.

It is strange, too, if Mr. Upshur's warning was honest, that
he spoke no surviving word of protest, undertook no recorded
action against officers when they entirely disregarded it. If
the ordeal Mackenzie faced was not rigged in his favor, what
was done by his sympathetic fellow professionals to temper
it had at least the appearance of fraudulence.

The commander, since he was being tried by court-martial,
already enjoyed under naval law numerous important advantages and privileges that would not have been his had he faced
action for murder in a criminal court.

Mackenzie was to be tried, not by a jury of civilians who
were probably antipathetic, but by thirteen brother officers.
Captain John Downes, who had sailed with Porter and Decatur, had been named by Upshur as president of the court. His
associate judges were ten captains and two commanders: salty
men, bronzed and brassbound, with the stain of their uniforms
in their bloodstreams. They were likely, when judging Mac-

kenzie, to put themselves in his place. When a brother officer was intemperately assailed by press and public, there was no question which way their sympathies would turn.

The defendant had other favorable handicaps, over and above the imperceptible whitewash his judges brought into court with them and, at the least opportunity, would be eager to apply. Court-martial procedure permitted a defendant to take the stand, or not, as he deemed best.

Mackenzie elected not to testify, yet by naval statute he still was allowed to submit written explanations to his judges without exposing himself to subsequent cross-examination. This was a point of obvious advantage to the navy's foremost author, and he was not backward in exploiting it. The harder he was pressed, the more he wrote.

For a man of martial calling, the commander was singularly reliant upon his pen. During the months of his ordeal, it seldom was entirely dry. The captain of the *Somers* surpassed even James W. Wales in zeal for revision and amendment. He had produced only two additional versions of his original statement. Mackenzie rewrote his own report three times.

The first brief dispatch that Gansevoort had borne to Washington had been followed by the expansion carried to the capital by the talkative young Perry. This longer narrative had been embellished, polished, and then submitted to Ogden Hoffman, recorder of the court of inquiry.

The executioner of Spencer, Cromwell, and Small composed a fourth justification of the hangings, which he included in his defense before the court-martial. He further favored that body with a series of written objections, interpolations, and interpretations. He concluded his literary-legal activity climactically in the blaze of verbiage that was his personally indited summation of his case.

For all his assiduous industry, the sailor-author left out a good deal that was pertinent. He compensated for these omissions by including much that was seldom encountered elsewhere in official communications.

Mackenzie, when put on trial for his life, chose to conduct his own defense. The commander in dress uniform would be a spectacle to hearten friendly witnesses and awe the hostile. Nevertheless, so that he should not lack expert legal guidance, the defendant retained as advisory counsel George Griffen and John Duer, a relative by marriage. The erstwhile captain of the *Somers*, furthermore, enjoyed a freedom rarely permitted a civilian accused of murder. Though removed from his command and technically under arrest, he was permitted to come and go pretty much as he pleased.

Inadvertently or otherwise, Upshur granted the defendant another considerable favor. The Secretary of the Navy was pleased to appoint as judge advocate, or prosecutor, William H. Norris, a Baltimore attorney; an unaggressive, even a plaintive man who collected a mass of grievances, many of them justified, as the trial progressed. These he sadly called to the court's attention but pressed his protests no further.

Norris was appointed so short a time before the court-martial convened that he had no time to prepare his case, and his mild nature apparently was awed by the panoplied high officers who sat in judgment. The judge advocate handled witnesses gingerly and never got his own attack started. Mackenzie might have had a poorer time of it if he had faced a more truculent opponent.

All the cited advantages to the commander and his cause were more or less legally sanctioned. He received further aid and comfort from other men who had no great respect for the law and none whatever for the orders contained in Upshur's letter to Jones. Mackenzie was helped materially from above, yet far more importantly from below.

In the hangings of Spencer, Cromwell, and Small, the principal officers of the *Somers* had been accessories before the fact. The verdict that Mackenzie at last had managed to squeeze out of his subordinates, in council assembled, had made them appear on the surface, at least, to be instigators of the triple execution. They had shared responsibility with their commander; they were as deeply implicated as he. It was evident, as the court-martial prepared to get under way, that if the defendant were found guilty, they would partake of his guilt and possibly of his punishment.

The not very bright officers of the brig had permitted her captain to lead them into deep trouble. By the time that became apparent to them, it was too late to backtrack. They could only follow Mackenzie further, in the hope that, having led them into the fire, he would get them back into the frying pan. Their support of their captain, therefore, necessarily was fervent and not overscrupulous. Only by getting him free, could they be certain of freedom for themselves.

It was these very men, these more than dubiously guilty officers, who were left in entire charge of the still-sequestered crew of the *Somers*.

Upshur had informed Commodore Jones that it was "*of the utmost importance that the crew of the* Somers *should be so kept as to prevent the possibility of any improper tampering with them.*" Upshur had told the commodore that "*too much caution cannot be used to ensure the exact truth in the testimony which the crew may be called upon to give.*"

Jones complied with the Secretary's directive imposing caution and vigilance by entrusting all the witnesses to the hang-

ings, save the eleven already jailed, to the care of those who
had recommended the executions.

Gansevoort now commanded the brig in Mackenzie's place.
The lieutenant and his associates were, by belief and by necessity, zealous supporters of the man about to be tried. Their
own testimony before the court-martial was to confirm his
principal contentions with well-drilled precision. They did
their rather frantic but effective best to enforce an equally
unscrupulous loyalty upon the *Somers'* crew. The gentlemen
of the quarter-deck were in a position to demand this, for they
had the naval officers' usual power to reward or punish the
enlisted personnel.

No one, including Mr. Upshur, seems to have been disturbed by this singular method of ensuring accurate testimony,
or by the highly prejudiced fashion in which Gansevoort commanded the brig.

Mackenzie's late subordinates were tirelessly active on his
behalf. They ransacked the vessel from stem to stern in the
hope of belatedly uncovering evidence that would justify the
hangings they had carried out two months earlier. They removed promising witnesses from the *Somers* and took them
to the home of Mackenzie's brother-in-law, there to be coached
in their forthcoming testimony by Mackenzie's attorneys.

The brig's officers violated the order of the Secretary of the
Navy as flagrantly as possible. They not only conditioned
witnesses-to-be; while so doing they also ignored Mr. Upshur's
exhortation to vigilance. Before the court-martial had been
long in session, several members of the *Somers'* crew whose
testimony might have been important walked away from the
brig, went over the hill, and were seen no more.

Mackenzie had further valuable support from his underlings. Nine members of his late command had been recommended by him for promotion in his second report to Upshur. Evidence that these would present before the court-martial was unlikely to be damaging to the defendant's case. If the commander were not honorably acquitted, the chances that the favorably cited nine would be advanced in rank were slight.

Everything that could be done to protect Alexander Slidell Mackenzie, as well as much that never should have been permitted, had been undertaken by the time the court-martial weighed anchor and deliberately made sail in an atmosphere already rank with duplicity, disobedience, and illegality. The air was not to freshen as the cruise progressed. At its outset the tribunal's destination became reasonably clear.

The commander's trial began aboard the receiving ship *North Carolina*, February 1, 1843. Five charges confronted the defendant. The first three accused him of murder aboard a United States vessel on the high seas, of oppression, of illegal punishment. A fourth, to be vacated during the trial, charged Mackenzie with mocking and taunting Philip Spencer immediately before his death. The fifth and final, also to be abandoned, alleged that the commander had treated his crew cruelly. The defendant pleaded not guilty to all charges.

At the beginning of the proceedings, Judge Advocate Norris lifted his voice in the first of the mild complaints that were to become chronic as the trial progressed. The Navy Department had neglected to furnish Norris with a list of the witnesses to be called. Therefore, he had had *"no opportunity of conversing with any of the witnesses, of whose names he is even entirely ignorant, except by rumor in respect to a few of them."*

A further break in the court's routine made still plainer the course that the thirteen judges planned to sail. On February 4, two lawyers appeared before the body and presented a petition. Benjamin F. Butler—not the malodorous Massachusetts politician but an eminent New Yorker who had been Andrew Jackson's attorney general—and Charles O'Connor had been retained by John Canfield Spencer. They now asked the judges' permission to appear officially in the trial of Mackenzie and to examine and cross-examine witnesses. Their petition ended:

"*The undersigned respectfully submit that the court has full power in its discretion to grant the application now made and that the nature of the investigation to be had, and the interest naturally and justly felt therein by those for whom they appear, render it proper that the same should be granted by the court.*"

It is indeterminable whether this was the elder Spencer's independent thrust or whether it had been undertaken with the encouragement of Mr. Upshur. Whatever the petition's impulse, the judges promptly and unanimously rejected it. The proceedings were to be strictly naval. Commander Mackenzie was to be tried by men of his profession and no others. With the necessary exception of the relatively inoffensive Mr. Norris, civilians were to be kept out.

The rejection must have disturbed the implacable spirit of John Canfield Spencer and have quickened the suspicion that, just possibly, he had been deceived by the Secretary of the Navy.

The court-martial moved from the receiving ship to the navy yard chapel on February 10, and continued to hold its sessions there until its final adjournment, April 1. Progress was slow, the weather was bad, and the proceedings were retarded further by illness. Mackenzie was bedridden for several days, and the health of one of the judges, Captain Joseph Smith, became so poor that he was excused from attendance.

The ponderous deliberation of the trial and its imperceptible daily advance toward a verdict joined hands with the innate inability of the American public to remain furiously indignant, week after week, about anything. These influences, in association, favored the defendant's cause. Popular denunciation dwindled and died away for lack of fuel.

The entire published record of Alexander Slidell Mackenzie's court-martial is jumbled and tediously repetitious. To newspaper readers of 1843, the day by day reports must have been patternless, static, and confusing. The testimony had not even novelty, since most of it was a warmed-over version of evidence that already had been presented to the court of inquiry.

Mackenzie, in the frequent written explanations he offered the court, referred irritably to time's passage and the innumerable delays. He may have been blind to the fact that these were, to some degree, his salvation. Men who lately had been bellowing for the commander's life now found as they read the account of still another day's proceedings that their mouths were spread by nothing more bloodthirsty than yawns.

The fact that the court-martial seemed to be going nowhere at an inconsiderable speed helped the defendant almost as much as his host of eagerly co-operative witnesses. These men, in their determination to support Mackenzie's every contention, never let veracity pull their testimony out of line.

Early in the trial the pliant James W. Wales offered a falsehood that set the pitch for countless misstatements, halftruths, and failures-to-recollect in subsequent witnesses' testimony. Wales's mendacity, if it had stood up under Norris' lukewarm cross-examination, would have helped the defendant materially.

The erstwhile purser's steward read aloud for the judges' benefit the last of his three divergent narratives concerning the fatal interview with Philip Spencer. He then, prompted by Mackenzie, added an apparently vital statement to the much-amended tale. The commander asked him:

"Did you or did you not understand from Mr. Spencer at what time the mutiny would break out?"

"He said," Wales replied promptly, *"very shortly and before our arrival in St. Thomas."*

This, if true, was important. It established the imminence of the uprising, excused to some extent the increasing fright of the *Somers'* officers, and lent the triple hanging at least a semblance of emergency. It was strange, though, that the witness had not remembered this potent fact until more than two months after Spencer was supposed to have confided it to him. It was stranger still that no one else aboard the brig had been told of a statement that fixed the time for the outbreak within narrow limits. On the night of Wales's interview with Spencer, the *Somers* was nine days' sailing time from St. Thomas.

An able cross-examiner could have butchered this compliant witness. Even so lenient a prosecutor as Judge Advocate Norris gave him a bad time.

Though he had recalled much of benefit to Mackenzie's case, Wales suffered an almost total lapse of memory on the witness stand. He reiterated, "I don't recollect," in response to Norris' unusually persistent questions, but at last, despite his twisting and dodging, the judge advocate got him into a corner where truthtelling was imperative.

"You say," Norris propounded, *"that you believe Com-*

mander Mackenzie knew the mutiny was to break out before the arrival at St. Thomas. What were your reasons for the belief?"

Wales and his falsehood collapsed together.

"I don't know," he bleated, *"that Commander Mackenzie did know it."*

He had done his best for his superior, who had recommended, in return, that the steward be promoted to the rank of purser. Mackenzie was a more successful prevaricator than his jackal. Since his statements to the court were presented in writing, Norris, by naval law, could not challenge them or cross-examine their author.

The court-martial, navigated by twelve experienced naval officers, now that Captain Smith's illness had retired him, was making heavy weather. It creaked, groaned, wallowed off its course, and laboriously got back onto it again. As week followed week, with the trial's conclusion not obviously nearer, the court began to wear the aspect of a permanent institution.

An apparently endless procession of witnesses succeeded each other. The testimony presented by most of the enlisted personnel was trivial. The *Somers'* officers had ransacked their command thoroughly and had painstakingly examined all members of the crew. Anyone found possessing anything—opinion, rumor, hearsay—that unselective minds considered evidential was hustled over to Commodore Perry's residence and there interviewed by counsel for the defense.

One thing distinguished the grab-bag collection of witnesses thus assembled, one universal quality. Among all the men and boys raked over by Mackenzie's volunteer assistants, no single being was found who, before Spencer's arrest, had ever heard mutiny discussed aboard the *Somers* or the word itself even mentioned.

Despite the officers' frantic search, nothing was uncovered that might be considered further proof of the guilt of Spencer, Cromwell, or Small, and in one instance the testimony of a witness backfired, to give an unexpected picture of the mental state of the council that had doomed three men.

William Collins had been stepped up from gunner's mate to boatswain's mate at the time of Cromwell's arrest. His loyal support of Mackenzie had inspired the commander to recommend his promotion to boatswain.

Collins had appeared as a witness before the officers' council on the day before the hangings. His testimony, taken down by Heiskill in the purser's own peculiar fashion, had included the following:

"Wishes Cromwell, Small and Spencer were out of the ship; thinks she would be more safe."

The council hastily presumed that this was the boatswain mate's delicate way of recommending that Spencer, Cromwell, and Small be put to death. On the witness stand, Collins informed the judge advocate that he had merely meant the brig would be more secure if the three men were set ashore.

"I was asked if I thought the ship would be safer with those men out of it and I said I did."

"What do you mean?" Norris demanded. *"Was not death spoken of?"*

"No, sir. They said 'out of the ship.' They did not say how they were to go out."

"Did you not understand," the judge advocate asked, still incredulously, *"that they were to be put to death in some form?"*

"No, sir."

The crew of the *Somers*, despite Upshur's exhortation to vigilance, was being depleted by desertions. Mackenzie's store of prisoners aboard the *North Carolina* was also dwindling. George Warner was among the first to be released. His jailers apparently did not consider him a sufficiently formidable mutineer to warrant their keeping him.

While the court-martial droned along, several other prisoners were let go, and additional were loosed when lawyers began habeas corpus proceedings on their behalf. Mackenzie held fast to McKee, McKinley, Wilson, and Green. The commander insisted they were to be tried for mutiny when his own ordeal had ended.

If the testimony of the *Somers'* enlisted men and boys was largely inconsequential, there were general characteristics that distinguished the evidence presented by all the brig's officers but one. The gentlemen of the quarter-deck endorsed all Mackenzie's defensive contentions. They agreed with him in reading a mutinous purpose into everything unusual that happened aboard the vessel during her five days of torment, no matter how ridiculous such reading sounded.

Judge Advocate Norris, cross-examining Sailing Master Perry, led him into a discussion of the relationship between Waltham, the wardroom steward, and Daniel McKinley, who reported him for offering McKinley stolen brandy. Perry previously had expressed the belief that both men had been potential mutineers.

"*And after this report,*" the judge advocate inquired, "*did you still believe that McKinley and he were accomplices of Mr. Spencer?*"

"I did," Perry answered stoutly, if with opaque logic. "*That was a particular reason for thinking so.*"

On the witness stand, the officers of the *Somers* were distinguished by their convenient ability to forget anything and everything that, if it were remembered, might weaken Mackenzie's case. Temporary Midshipman Wales was adept in practicing these advantageous lapses, but Lieutenant Gansevoort's appropriate black-outs of memory surpassed even his.

Under cross-examination by Norris, the lieutenant's mind became almost entirely blank. He could not recall whether, during his conversation with Small, he had asked the little man if an actual plot to take the brig was developing. He could not remember asking his informant for the names of other mutineers. He could not recollect offering Small any inducement to make a complete confession.

When it came to a discussion of his talk with Spencer, Gansevoort's memory grew, if possible, worse.

Had he asked the number and the names of Spencer's enlisted accomplices? "*I don't recollect.*"

Had he inquired whether the conspiracy was still operative? "*I don't recollect.*"

Had he asked when Small had joined the plot? "*I don't recollect.*"

Had he inquired when the Greek Paper had been composed? "*I don't recollect.*"

Had he demanded of Small whether "E. Andrews" was his real name? "*I don't recollect.*"

Had he asked Spencer whether all those listed on the Greek Paper had knowledge of the conspiracy? "*Not that I recollect.*"

Gansevoort on the witness stand could recall so little of what he had said, or had not said, that what he had forgotten might have been more important than the minimum he managed to remember.

Young Dr. Leecock was less successful than his colleagues in recollecting only what best would serve the interests of Mackenzie—and of his officers. A unique integrity, or sensitivity, made the surgeon unable to deny brazenly what he knew was the truth, however damaging verity might be to the commander's defense.

Among the seven officers who composed the council that decreed the hangings, Leecock alone was able to recall that Mackenzie had sent the body, via Gansevoort, a peremptory order to hurry along its verdict. After Spencer's execution, the captain of the *Somers* had informed his crew that the boy had been lying during the last hour of his life. All the brig's officers had been deaf at that moment, save Leecock. He tried under cross-examination to be as loyally mendacious as they—and failed.

Norris asked the surgeon whether he had heard Mackenzie say *"anything about Mr. Spencer's truth or falsehood"* and Leecock replied with the standard response of *Somers'* officers under cross-questioning: *"I don't recollect."*

"Did you not," the judge advocate insisted, *"hear any such expression as this: 'That young man died with lies in his mouth'?"*

Leecock did his best.

"No, sir. I did not hear that expression; I heard nothing of that kind."

"Did you hear any statement that Mr. Spencer had been telling the commander falsehoods before he died?"

"I think," the surgeon faltered, his hardihood collapsing, *"I did hear some such observation as that."*

The men and boys, still held aboard the *Somers* and still under the command of Gansevoort and his fellow officers, provided favorable, if somewhat glib, testimony for the commander. The enlisted personnel were well aware by now on

which side their bread was buttered. Occasionally, their eager-
ness to be helpful was an embarrassment to the defense.

Frederick Snyder, second-class apprentice, appeared as witness for Mackenzie but got disastrously off the track he had
been drilled to follow. Under direct examination by the commander, Snyder testified that he had heard Spencer ask Cromwell whether the *Somers* could be turned into a slave runner.
Cromwell had replied that, with some alterations, the brig
might qualify.

"*Did Mr. Spencer ask Cromwell,*" Mackenzie inquired cor-
rectively, "*how she would do for a* slaver, *or a* pirate?"

"*Yes, sir,*" the witness replied, making hurried amends. "*For
a slaver or a pirate. He said both.*"

Snyder, cross-examined, admitted that he had lately deserted
from the *Somers* but had been recaptured.

"*Have you been punished for it?*" the judge advocate asked.

"*No, sir; not yet,*" the witness answered a little frantically.
"*I do not know whether Mr. Spencer said 'slaver' or 'pirate.' I
can't recollect which one. He said one or the other.*"

Mackenzie had still further allies. The *Courier and Enquirer*, property of his neighbor, continued to support him loyally. Most of the Whig newspapers originally had favored the
commander, though as weeks crept by they were paying less
and less attention in news and editorial columns to an apparently interminable trial.

Mackenzie also had at least one still-implacable enemy.
Midway through the court-martial, John Canfield Spencer
struck again at the slayer of his son.

CHAPTER 15

Restoration

"A flagrant act of injustice and inhumanity, like that committed by Commander Mackenzie and his associates, cannot be done with impunity."—JAMES FENIMORE COOPER.

THE COURT-MARTIAL'S deliberate progress, a growing popular belief that Mackenzie's judges intended eventually to set him free, exhausted the last vestige of tolerance in a chronically impatient man. The elder Spencer had believed, with a good deal of encouragement from Abel P. Upshur, that the erstwhile captain of the *Somers* could safely be left for punishment in the hands of the Navy Department.

The trite testimony of well-schooled witnesses and the strong smell of whitewash that permeated the proceedings had convinced the Secretary of War that naval hands, in this instance, were more inclined to protect than chastise. To John Canfield Spencer's unabated craving for vengeance there now was added the galling suspicion that he had been duped. At that bitter moment, he would have sacrificed much to have been in the judge advocate's place.

Norris would have welcomed the substitution and would gladly have yielded his office. He was being thwarted; he was being denied what he considered a judge advocate's rightful privileges. The plaintive protests he uttered were graciously received by Mackenzie's judges, and then ignored.

The officers at the navy yard had placed an entirely one-sided interpretation upon Mr. Upshur's pre-court-martial admonition. The Secretary had warned against "improper tampering" with members of the *Somers'* crew. Authority had resolved immediately that any association between the judge advocate and the brig's company would be the height of impropriety.

This biased arrangement roused Norris on March 8 to another customarily mild complaint. He had done his best to prepare the prosecution's case, but he had got no help from anyone. Attempts he had made to interview *Somers'* officers had been dismayingly unsuccessful. The judge advocate had tried to question Midshipman Hays and Acting Midshipman Tillotson. Both young men had told him politely but firmly that they did not wish to talk to him.

"All the officers and crew of that brig," Norris complained to the court, *"were furnished by the department for witnesses at my selection. With neither have I had any opportunities for conversation."*

The court complaisantly accepted his statement, but it still kept him away from the *Somers,* her officers, and her enlisted men and boys. This and other prejudiced conduct of the tribunal blew upon the perpetually smoldering coals of John Canfield Spencer's wrath and rewhetted his original intention.

The court's treatment of Norris rankled in the judge advocate's usually placid bosom, too, and the conviction that he was being misused brought about on March 9 the only row that disturbed the torpid tribunal from its now remote beginning until its still-distant conclusion.

Oliver H. Perry was on the stand. In the months that had elapsed since he had told Upshur that Spencer, during his last hour, had dictated to Mackenzie a farewell message, young

Perry had acquired a warier nature and a salutary reticence. His responses to Norris' cross-examination were as brief and non-committal as possible.

The judge advocate questioned the witness with unwonted persistence concerning the existence of this disputed message while Mackenzie twisted in his chair, fumed, and grew red.

"*Did you*," Norris demanded, "*hear Mr. Spencer say he could not write with his irons on?*"

"No, sir."

"*Did Mr. Spencer take the pen and try to write?*"

"*I did not see him.*"

"*Did you hear the commander tell him he would write for him?*"

"No, sir."

This verbal hammering of his nephew finally broke the commander's composure and wrung from him the only impromptu utterance he voiced during the entire trial. Mackenzie sprang from his chair and strode forward, scarlet and furious, to confront the judge advocate.

"*Why*," the affronted man cried, stung in what was still a sensitive area, "*do you ask this question about Mr. Spencer not being able to write in irons? He declined to write.*"

Norris gaped for an instant, then summoned all his own small truculence.

"*Yes, sir*," he retorted, "*but I am told he afterward dictated to you what to write.*"

For a moment, while the astounded court-martial recovered breath, the two men vocally belabored each other, Mackenzie angrily insisting that his official report had contained all that Spencer had ever told him, Norris stubbornly maintaining his belief that the boy had dictated a further farewell message that never had been delivered.

Until that violent passage, no trial for murder could have been more harmonious. The judges, reviving from their stupefaction, intervened, parted the disputants, and restored order. On the following day, Mackenzie, once more the composed and confident defendant, submitted a written statement to the court.

This maintained that the only words addressed by Spencer to his parents had been included in the commander's report. That report had quoted the boy as speaking fondly of his family and regretting his past *"crimes."*

"The message of Mr. Spencer to his friends," Mackenzie's explanation concluded, *"was communicated to the secretary of the navy as the least painful mode that occurred to Commander Mackenzie of making it known to them."*

It was while the commander was sore and shaken by this outburst that John Canfield Spencer tried to get at him again.

The Secretary of War still wanted to see Mackenzie hanged. On March 10, the elder Spencer made a desperate last attempt to pry his enemy away from the benign court-martial and hale him before a civilian tribunal that would try him more briskly and inconsiderately for murder.

Counsel for Spencer and counsel for the commander appeared on March 10 in the chambers of the same Judge Betts who had denied Margaret Cromwell's earlier appeal for a warrant against Mackenzie and Gansevoort, charging them with murder on the high seas. The opposing attorneys wrangled heatedly over the question of whether a grand jury legally could indict for murder a man already on trial for that crime.

Betts promised to render a decision on March 20. There may have been no connection between the looming danger and the fact that on March 15 and 16 the court-martial suspended its proceedings because Mackenzie was too ill to attend.

Judge Betts ruled on the appointed date that, under the circumstances, the grand jury had no jurisdiction. Obstructed again in his craving for retribution, John Canfield Spencer now could only bide his time and hope, without conviction, that the court-martial would punish Alexander Slidell Mackenzie fittingly.

The trial of the commander went on still more deliberately, as though it could not stop until its flagging momentum had entirely failed. There were no further lively moments, no more quarrels to enliven the sessions. The court-martial and the public interest in it were running down together.

If the more than leisurely pace set by the tribunal had been purposely designed to smother earlier and uproarious popular indignation toward the defendant in particular and naval brutality in general, the stratagem had been an unqualified success.

Most newspapers had already discontinued day by day reports of the trial. Their readers did not protest the omission. The proceedings, which had begun to the accompaniment of sound and fury, were expiring unmourned in a heavy atmosphere of boredom.

Indifference was afflicting all concerned, save possibly the defendant, and even his worries over the outcome of the ordeal could not have been acute. He was too complacently self-righteous a man ever to believe that his brother officers would punish him for what had been, plainly, his manifest duty.

Toward the court-martial's conclusion Mackenzie's friend, Colonel Webb, tried to pump oxygen into a dying story by publishing in the *Courier and Enquirer* a series of articles, signed "Pinckney," to the glorification of the commander and the defamation of his enemies. Their tone was so vituperative that the *Herald* commented:

"There never has been a better exhibition of the violence, absurdity and gross scurrility of the party press. . . . The relatives of the accused have been attacked; the government has been attacked; the judge advocate has been attacked. Everyone, in fine, that refused to approve of the entire course pursued by Commander Mackenzie has been attacked in the most ferocious manner."

No one else seems to have shared James Gordon Bennett's indignation. The *Somers* case had first been brought to general attention in mid-December, and here it was late March. People were sick of the whole apparently endless problem.

On March 21, the trial came to a halt with the abruptness of a ship running aground on a sand bar. The proceedings could have gone on still longer. There were a number of witnesses who had not yet been heard. Inertia, not logic, stopped the court-martial. Everyone concerned in it had had enough—except Alexander Slidell Mackenzie.

On the following day, the commander presented to the tribunal the last and most elegant of the communications he had written for its enlightenment. Mr. Griffen, of counsel, read the production aloud, but Mackenzie himself had indited it. He had embodied in the composition all that was most striking in his art. In this unsuccinct summation of his defense, the sailor-author depended more on eloquence than evidence.

The essay included a number of contentions that Mackenzie hitherto had forgotten to mention, and corrected several of his earlier convictions. In his report to Upshur, the commander had demoted Spencer from his original post as chief mutineer-to-be and had elected Daniel McKinley in his place as *"the individual who, if the mutiny had been successful, would have made away with all his competitors and risen to command."*

In his summation, Mackenzie rejected McKinley and chose Cromwell—by what measurement he forgot to explain—as *"the master spirit of tumult and death."* He, *"clothed with a sort of evil ubiquity, was to interpose his malign counsel and giant strength wherever they should be most needed."* Cromwell never had been forgiven for his profane comment concerning the jib lacing Mackenzie had invented.

The defendant, in his peroration, reached heights probably never attained before or since in naval official communications.

"Suppose," he implored the court, *"that the Somers, now turned pirate, while cruising off our coast, had been permitted by Heaven in an evil hour to capture some vessel plying between this country and Europe, freighted with the talent and beauty of the land.*

"The men are all murdered and the females, including perhaps the new-made wife and maidens just blooming into womanhood, are forced to become the brides of pirates. A universal shriek of agony bursts from the American people throughout all their vast domains and the wailing is echoed back from the whole civilized world.

"And where then could the commander of the Somers have hidden his head, branded as it would have been by a mark of infamy as indelible as that stamped upon the forehead of Cain?"

Alexander Slidell Mackenzie included in his opus several respectfully admiring references to the flag of his country.

Anticlimax necessarily succeeded this literary eruption. The judge advocate's summation, which dealt primly with the points of law at issue, was by comparison a wan and gray performance.

During the next five days, all the testimony produced during the trial—the whole soggy, conglomerate poundage—was read aloud to the judges, who on March 28 retired to debate and ballot on their verdict. Their findings were not immediately announced but were forwarded to Washington for approval by the Secretary of the Navy before publication.

The judges sent their verdict to Upshur, March 28. On March 31, young Dr. Leecock, momentarily alone in the wardroom of the *Somers*, pressed the muzzle of a pistol against his forehead and pulled the trigger. He had been suffering, the *Tribune* reported next morning, from "*settled melancholy and partial derangement induced by a long and severe attack of yellow fever.*" How much of that explanation was furnished by the ready officers aboard the brig, how much the memory of three who were hanged inclined the surgeon to suicide, no one can tell.

Passed Assistant Surgeon Richard W. Leecock was twenty-eight years old and a native of Norfolk, Virginia. The *Tribune*'s brief account of his death made no attempt to link it to the recently concluded trial of Alexander Slidell Mackenzie, yet Leecock, when he had testified before the court-martial, had displayed a tenderness of mind and a fundamental honesty that had distinguished him from other, less conscientious officer witnesses.

Recollection of the executions of Spencer, Cromwell, and Small and of the disreputable officers' council that authorized the hangings must have been one of the influences that impelled an ailing and regretful man to end his own life at the court-martial's conclusion.

Mackenzie's tribunal held its final session April 1, exactly two months after its initial convention, four months and a day after McKinley, McKee, Green, and Wilson had been clapped into irons aboard the *Somers*.

Judge Advocate Norris had informed Secretary Upshur of the court's impending end, and he, in turn, had written to ask what charges were to be brought against the four prisoners. Norris, this morning of April 1, told the judges that he had frequently suggested without result that Mackenzie prefer charges against McKinley, McKee, Wilson, and Green. The judge advocate had come to believe that the commander had no intention of doing so.

No enlightenment could be obtained from the defendant, for he was not present. Norris informed the judges he had sent a provost marshal to bring Mackenzie in and then had learned that the commander *"was absent at his residence in the country, thirty miles distant."*

The court thereupon permanently adjourned. The four captives, after long imprisonment for no formally specified crime, were allowed to go free.

The last two charges against Alexander Slidell Mackenzie, accusing him of conduct unbecoming an officer and of unnecessary cruelty, had been abandoned by the judge advocate during the trial. The judges of the court-martial, reduced to twelve by Smith's illness, were required to ballot upon the first three accusations. Two-thirds of the votes cast were requisite for a verdict on each charge.

On charge one, alleging willful murder, three judges found the defendant guilty; nine, not guilty.

On the second charge, which accused the commander of "oppression," four voted Mackenzie guilty; eight, not guilty.

The judges unanimously found the defendant not guilty of the final allegation, which maintained that he had inflicted punishment illegally.

The navy took care of its distinguished officer, let whitewash spatter where it might. The commander had been cleared on all counts, but by law his judges had a further duty to perform. They were now obliged to vote on whether Mackenzie should be *honorably* acquitted or released without that adjective's grace.

The court's already overextended clemency could be stretched no further. The vote was three for honorable, nine for less creditable acquittal.

The verdict of the court-martial, published in Washington on April 19, roused little general interest. Men who once had bellowed for the commander's death told each other now: "They've found Mackenzie, that fellow who hanged what's-his-name, not guilty," and then went on to livelier discussion of Daniel Webster's retirement from the cabinet and of Tyler's forming intention to run for president again.

The *Herald* already had taken the edge off the official announcement by printing the story of the acquittal eight days earlier, but to one embittered elder the exculpating verdict was a blow, no less enraging for being half-expected. It canceled irrevocably the vengeful tribute John Canfield Spencer still had hoped to pay his slain son; it set the always simmering wrath of the Secretary of War to seething.

He had been craftily prevailed upon and massively deceived

by an associate, by a fellow member of the President's official family. Upshur had induced a bereaved father to leave punishment of his enemy to the Navy Department, and now that the murderous commander had been acquitted, he doubtless was smugly pleased. He would learn at the first opportunity that no one flouted John Canfield Spencer with impunity.

The Secretary of War carried his new enmity into a cabinet meeting and there, before his startled colleagues, intemperately denounced the chicanery of the Secretary of the Navy. The *Tribune* got wind of the quarrel and reported cautiously:

"It would seem from the rumors from various quarters that there has been some personal quarrel in the cabinet between Secretaries Spencer and Upshur and that it may have been connected with the case of Mackenzie. The Washington correspondent of 'The Baltimore Patriot' states that the decision of the court martial was submitted to the cabinet on Wednesday and that Mr. Spencer was present at the meeting. It is rumored through the streets of Washington that sharp words passed between him and Secretary Upshur on the subject."

John Canfield Spencer's outburst may have relieved an immediate pressure, yet, being a lawyer, he must have recognized that his last chance for vengeance had gone. The court-martial's verdict had put his enemy beyond the reach of any reprisal less lawless than Mackenzie's own had been.

Released and secure, Alexander Slidell Mackenzie was resting after long travail in his North Tarrytown home, above the shining plane of the Tappan Zee. If the lukewarm verdict had disappointed him, if he felt that his shining rectitude had been faintly dimmed, there were many compensations to soothe the mind of a sailor, home from a murder trial.

Mackenzie's farm would be responsive to its owner's care; Mr. Irving and his famous friends were close at hand. And

above these advantages, there was peace here—reassuring, healing peace and security. The commander was safe at last, safe
from the sourceless, degrading dread that had impelled him to
hang three men; safe from the menace of the law; safe in his
social position and naval rank; safe from the vengeance of the
elder Spencer; safe in the arms of Abel P. Upshur.

CHAPTER 16

Aftermath

"The acquitted and applauded man withdrew to a lonely retreat . . . and was only roused from his depression to give signs of a diseased mind."—THOMAS HART BENTON.

ALEXANDER SLIDELL MACKENZIE'S tribulation had ended, and it may have been that he regretted it. His ordeal would have been dangerously depleting to a man of ordinary fiber, but the commander was compounded of uncommon materials. This being so, it is possible that, among all those who had been subjected to the extended strain of the murder trial, the defendant had most nearly enjoyed himself.

There had been advantages to the court-martial counterbalancing the fact that the commander's life had been moderately in jeopardy. His singular nature demanded an audience. When no better was available, he frequently served as his own. It may have been this desire for popular attention that had turned him to authorship as an avocation.

While the trial had crept forward, Mackenzie must have had an appeasing sense of importance; an agreeable awareness that he was the most closely observed person in the chapel courtroom. His situation as defendant had another recommendation that would appeal strongly to a writing man: whatever the commander penned for the court's benefit was certain of publication and bound to command at least a limited number of readers.

The *Tribune* shared the sailor-author's opinion of the florid summation of the defense he composed, and issued it in pamphlet form (price, 12½ cents). Mackenzie autographed copies and distributed them among his friends.

Though the court-martial had found him mildly blameworthy, it is unlikely that this depressed a phenomenally self-righteous man; nor is it probable that recollection of the triple hanging kept him awake of nights. The commander was sublimely sure of his rectitude, as only an intensely vain, completely humorless man could be.

No shadow but his own accompanied Mackenzie about his riverside farm or followed him to "Sunnyside," where he continued to enjoy *"the favor and acquaintance of some distinguished individuals."* It is a pity that Charles Dickens was not among them.

That perceptive gentleman, after measuring the commander, might have added still another portrait to an immortal gallery: a picture containing traces of a more homicidal Pecksniff, a touch of a more prudish Micawber, and much singular material derived from Alexander Slidell Mackenzie's own unique self.

Mortal minds forever expect to discover recompense and equity in a world conspicuously understocked with either. Humanity clings with pathetic optimism to the unwarranted belief that evil inevitably is punished and virtue as certainly is rewarded. Blinding themselves to inconvenient reality, men continued to search for poetic justice in matters devoid of any justice whatever. Rather than admit that their quest fails, they fashion consoling legends.

During the century plus since the *Somers* tragedy, myths and semifictions have burgeoned to blur the true outline of the event and its aftermath. Some of these distortions seem to have been spontaneously created; others have been contrived by identifiable hands. A few may be partly factual; many contain no trace of verity.

The romantically inclined enemies of Alexander Slidell Mackenzie were compelled to exercise much ingenuity and to display more than the mythmakers' usual disregard of facts in providing for the executioner of Spencer, Cromwell, and Small a fate that would gratify moralists. The more frequently employed blackings would not stick to the commander's reputation. He was a highly moral man himself.

It was ridiculous to allege that remorse drove this conspicuously prim person to dissipation, or that a lifelong teetotaler drowned himself in liquor. There remained one disparagement that might apply, and this only after a wholesale disregard of the facts. A more than usually questionable legend recites that the memory of his fell deed drove Mackenzie mad.

The original author of this fiction cannot be identified, but the tale pleased popular fancy, and in later years it was caught up and elaborated by many persons who should have known better.

Senator Thomas Hart Benton of Missouri wrote in his memoirs:

"The acquitted and applauded man withdrew to a lonely retreat, oppressed with gloom and melancholy, visible only to a few and was only roused from his depression to give signs of a diseased mind."

More misstatement seldom has been packed into a single sentence, and the supporting evidence Benton presents is self-destructive. Nevertheless, he upheld the romantic proprieties by transforming Mackenzie into a lunatic.

If the commander were deranged, his was a singular mania.

It did not bar him from the continued successful practice of both his profession and his avocation. Most men of indubitable sanity accomplish less in their entire lives than the sailor-author did in the remainder of his.

Mackenzie did not return to the *Somers* after his acquittal but was assigned to ordnance duty. He found time and energy during this period to continue his writing. His *Life of Commodore Stephen Decatur* was published in 1846. On May 25 of that same year, President Polk entrusted to him a delicate diplomatic mission.

The Mexican trouble, long simmering on the back of the national stove, had boiled over at last into a war that nobody wanted. Taylor was across the Rio Grande, and the fleet had blockaded Vera Cruz, but Polk was eager to settle the conflict by cash, not carnage.

The Mexican government remained intransigent, but it was tottering, and Antonio Lopez de Santa Anna, the deposed and exiled dictator, waited hopefully in Havana for its collapse. Polk thought it possible that a deal might be made with him.

It was the President's idea that, if Santa Anna could be persuaded to undertake a coup, the navy would let him through the blockade. Thereafter, when he had seized the government and a little face-saving powder had been burned, a negotiated peace might be contrived, with the United States paying liberally for whatever territory it took.

The man chosen to sell this scheme to the erstwhile dictator would need intelligence, resolution, and tact. Polk selected as his envoy Alexander Slidell Mackenzie. The commander spoke Spanish. Moreover, his brother, John Slidell, had been minister to Mexico. These facts must have been influential, but the President certainly had other reasons for his choice. The alleged progressive insanity of Mackenzie would have disqualified him immediately, yet Benton sticks to his story.

According to the Senator, the commander preserved the secrecy his errand required by arraying himself in his dress uniform—that, at least, was in character—and by driving spectacularly through the streets of Havana in an open carriage at midday and thence to Santa Anna's hacienda. There, Benton writes, Mackenzie behaved so eccentrically that his host rejected the proposal. When his visitor had been shown the door, Santa Anna turned to his secretary and demanded scornfully:

"*Why has the President sent me this fool?*"

That is the way Benton relates it. He was not present at the Mackenzie–Santa Anna interview, nor does he mention who told him about it. The Senator's tale, at best, could have been only hearsay and established facts shoot it completely to pieces.

The need for secrecy, which Benton emphasizes, could not have been extreme. Several days before the commander left for Havana, the *Philadelphia Ledger* had printed a full account of his contemplated mission, Finally and positively, the exiled dictator did not flout Mackenzie's proposal. The envoy was successful, despite Benton's jeers, in persuading Santa Anna, who, in August of 1846, was passed through the American blockade and landed at Vera Cruz.

If subsequently the dictator went back on the agreement he had made in Havana, double-crossed Polk, and lost the war, the flaw was in Santa Anna's mentality, not in Mackenzie's.

The commander, his diplomatic errand accomplished, had sailed from Havana to join the blockading fleet. Nothing in his record thenceforth is symptomatic of that mental decay his wishful enemies discerned.

Mackenzie served as fleet ordnance officer during the siege of Vera Cruz. He was one of the navy's representatives at the city's formal surrender. He commanded land batteries at the storming of Tabasco and was detailed to ordnance duty with the home squadron early in 1847.

On August 27, 1847, Mackenzie became captain of the steam sloop *Mississippi,* later to be brother-in-law Matthew Calbraith Perry's flagship on his visit to Japan. The commander served aboard the vessel until April 21, 1848, when he was granted three months' leave and returned to his North Tarrytown farm.

Mackenzie had been restored to the family and friends whom he mentioned so frequently in his public utterances. In a tranquil resort of the cultured and socially important, the *Somers* tragedy, the strange terror that had possessed the brig, the triple execution that had exorcised it, must have become to a complacent memory an episode scarcely to be distinguished from the many others the commander had crowded into an uncommonly full life. Time's lengthening perspective minimized and mellowed them all.

The sailor-author did not fritter away his leave in idleness. He worked upon the manuscript of still another book: *A Journal of a Tour of Ireland.* It never was to be published. The one-time captain of the *Somers* was a diligent person and unlikely to be haunted by the past. He never laid aside his armor of self-righteousness. His piety, excessive even for his time, impelled him to draw from any enterprise edifying and improving homilies.

It is doubtful whether Alexander Slidell Mackenzie, that egocentric man, could have been altered in nature by anything less than death itself. This came to him at his home on September 13, 1848, in his forty-seventh year.

The father's reputed insanity did not mar the energies or abilities of his children. One son, Ranald, was graduated from West Point in 1862, and before the Civil War had ended, had risen to the command of all the cavalry in the Army of the James. A younger, Alexander, Jr., served meritoriously in the navy from 1855 until he was killed by natives on Formosa in 1867.

Legend has done its worst, too, for Guert Gansevoort, Mackenzie's faithful lieutenant and echo. On him has been imposed the tale of contrition-through-alcoholism that never could be stretched to fit his superior. Myth maintains that from the day of the three-ply execution onward, Gansevoort knew neither success nor happiness but was hounded downhill by the furies into a drunkard's grave.

There is substance of a sort to this yarn, as there is to the story of Mackenzie's madness, since in each instance an identified person sponsored the legend.

Thurlow Weed was proprietor of the *Albany Evening Journal* and an orthodox Whig. For political reasons, and perhaps personal, he was one of the many enemies of John Canfield Spencer. The Gansevoort family were from Albany.

As Weed tells the story in his autobiography, on December 21, 1842, which was seven days after the *Somers* had returned from her tragic cruise, he was in Philadelphia and fell in with an old familiar. This was Passed Midshipman Gansevoort (Christian name not given), who was a cousin of Guert's.

Officer and journalist dined and drank together and before the convivial evening ended, Midshipman Gansevoort confided that he had spent the previous evening with Lieutenant Gansevoort, who had been carrying Mackenzie's first dispatch to Secretary Upshur. Guert and his cousin had made merry and toward the end of the revel, the lieutenant had told the midshipman a tale that the latter confided to Weed *"as a friend of them and their families."*

According to Lieutenant Gansevoort, who told Midshipman Gansevoort, who told Thurlow Weed, who included the story in a book published almost forty years later, the officers' council aboard the *Somers*, after long debate, had been unable to reach a verdict. The lieutenant had gone on deck and had told Mackenzie so.

Thereupon, still according to the much relayed tale, Mackenzie said that the witnesses could not have been properly examined. He gave the lieutenant an additional list of questions that should be asked them and sent him below again. Later, Gansevoort returned to the deck and told the commander that the council still could not make up its collective mind. As Weed remembered it, years afterward, Midshipman Gansevoort then quoted his cousin, thus:

"Captain Mackenzie replied that it was evident that these young men had wholly misapprehended the nature of the evidence, if they had not also misapprehended the aggravated character of the offense and that there would be no security for the lives of officers nor protection to commerce if an example was not made in a case so flagrant as this. It was my duty, he urged, to impress these views upon the court.

"I returned and did, by impressing these considerations, obtain a reluctant conviction of the accused."

Weed writes that later, when Mackenzie was on trial, he tried to reach the elder Spencer and tell him the story, but the Secretary of War refused to see him. Soon thereafter Midshipman Gansevoort was lost at sea.

The next summer, Weed says, he dined with Guert Gansevoort in Boston and sat with him over hot whisky punch until the small hours. The newspaperman spoke of the evening he had spent with Guert's cousin and, when questioned, repeated all that Midshipman Gansevoort had told him concerning the *Somers* case. Gansevoort thereupon sprang up and rushed from the room without a word of farewell. Weed continues:

"In the last years of his life, when he was stationed at The Brooklyn Navy Yard, then a sad wreck of his former self, he came frequently to see me, but was always moody, taciturn and restless."

Weed contended that *"a bright, intelligent, high-principled and sensitive gentleman and a most promising officer of the navy spent the best part of his life, a prey to unavailing remorse."*

The lurid tale does not hang together. It all is double hearsay, related long after the event, and many of its details are incorrect. Guert Gansevoort's reputed meeting with his cousin, December 20, 1842, plainly is misdated.

The lieutenant left New York with Mackenzie's first report, December 14th. He could scarcely have been no further on his way than Philadelphia six days later.

There are further discrepancies. The alcoholic wreck that Guert Gansevoort allegedly became distinguished himself as captain of the sloop *John Adams* during the Mexican War. He served ably thereafter with the Pacific Squadron and was then chief of ordnance at the Brooklyn Navy Yard until the Civil War began. He commanded the ironclad *Roanoke* and other vessels during the conflict and was retired as commodore in 1867, after forty-five years of active service.

Gansevoort's naval record does not fit the picture of a guilt-ridden sot that is painted by Weed's unconfirmed narrative.

The subsequent career of the brig *Somers* is obscured by

still grislier myth. She was a poorly designed, dangerously top-heavy craft, but legend has added much more to her detriment. After the hangings, so the tale runs, the *Somers* became a haunted ship, a devil brig with the ghosts of the unjustly hanged gibbering nightly in her shrouds, and her fell career was appropriately ended when she rolled over and sank with all on board.

The prison and the gallows of Philip Spencer, Samuel Cromwell, and Elisha Small was a short-lived craft, it is true, but her untimely demise was due less to malignant occult forces than to faulty construction. On December 8, 1846, the cranky brig capsized and sank, carrying down with her, not her entire crew, but forty of her complement of ninety men.

Among the rescued was the *Somers'* then captain, Raphael Semmes, later to command the Confederate commerce raiders, the *Sumter* and the *Alabama*.

Though the general response to the verdict of Mackenzie's court-martial had been profound indifference, the *Somers* scandal nevertheless supplied a reaction that very gradually increased in strength. The furore that the triple hangings originally aroused had shocked and disturbed the hitherto respected United States Navy. During the limited period of intense popular indignation, the service had received more abuse than in all its earlier existence.

Some of this execration, forward-looking officers admitted privately to each other, was merited. The navy had become a lamentably static, not to say stagnant, institution. Something should be done to prevent young wastrels like Philip Spencer from becoming midshipmen. It was time that the service ceased to serve as a school of correction for youthful incorrigibles. Something might even be done to take the training

of future officers out of the less than dexterous hands of men
like Alexander Slidell Mackenzie.

Most of these concessions were hush-hush. The navy and
naval practices had been so intemperately defamed by an overheated populace that further open criticism by its own officers
would have been so much lily-gilding. Nevertheless, an im-
petus toward reform had been born of the deaths of Spencer,
Cromwell, and Small, and this new force never entirely failed
in the years immediately following.

Mackenzie's court-martial and its prejudiced outcome had
opened an aperture, and through it thoughtful men had been
able to see the archaic rigidity of a service that was dominated
by shellbacked commodores who had forgotten little and
learned less since their own distant entrance into the navy.

Brassbound authorities continued to maintain that what
had been good enough for them in the way of training was
still adequate for young officers-to-be, and Congress, no radical
institution itself, readily had agreed.

The military academy at West Point had been established
in 1802, but all subsequent attempts to set up a similar professional institution for midshipmen had been thwarted by
congressmen and commodores. The shore schools maintained
by the navy in New York, Boston, and Norfolk were staffed
largely by political appointees. These "naval asylums" were
designed primarily to keep youngsters out of trouble between
their periods of sea service. Education was secondary.

In 1838, still another school for midshipmen had been established in Philadelphia. At its beginning, it did not diverge from
the norm already fixed by its predecessors, but in 1841, William Chauvenet, Yale graduate, mathematician, astronomer,
and inspired teacher, was appointed to the new establishment,
which immediately responded to his influence. Contrary to

precedent, the Philadelphia school began to educate its students thoroughly in the theory of their profession. A pattern vaguely outlined by the aftermath of the *Somers* tragedy was beginning to form.

Further impulsion, determined yet delicate, was required, and a little man with oversized whiskers supplied it. In 1845. George Bancroft, historian and educator, became President Polk's Secretary of the Navy. He, like other reflective men, had been disturbed by the deficiencies in the service that the *Somers* affair had revealed. Bancroft must have already thought long and hard concerning reform in the navy's educational system, for his subsequent procedure showed no trace of hesitation.

The new Secretary was aware that frontal assault upon congressional reluctance to establish a naval academy promised little. Instead of bucking the line, he made an end run. Bancroft had studied the laws that applied to the problem and knew exactly where he stood. He needed no enabling legislation for his plan.

The statutes authorized the Secretary of the Navy to fix the place where midshipmen on shore duty should wait further orders, and there to provide them with adequate instruction. Bancroft discussed his purpose with William L. Marcy, Secretary of War, and with William Chauvenet. Thereafter, the new Secretary of the Navy moved rapidly and purposefully.

There was a crumbling army post, Fort Severn, on Windmill Point, Annapolis, Maryland. Marcy turned this over to the Navy Department. Bancroft scrapped the "naval asylums" at Boston, New York, Norfolk, Philadelphia, and shipped all the young men who had been in these establishments to Fort Severn. Henceforth, he announced, this was to be the United

States Naval School. Chauvenet was the foremost member of the faculty Bancroft assembled.

The reform was accomplished within the framework of existing law and with the funds already at the command of the Secretary of the Navy. When the new congress assembled, the alteration in the navy's educational system was an accomplished fact. In 1850-51, the national legislature transformed the Naval School into the United States Naval Academy. Thus, the impulse roused by a triple hanging on the brig *Somers*, joining with others, had fulfilled its original dim intention.

George Bancroft was the father of the professional school at Annapolis, but Alexander Slidell Mackenzie, in association with Philip Spencer, was among the academy's remoter forebears.

CHAPTER 17

Autopsy

"Though the principal perpetrator ... has safely passed the ordeal of a court martial—to the wonder of all who have read the testimony—the blood of the slain cries from out the deep and sooner or later will be heard, no matter what attempts are made to stifle it."—JAMES FENIMORE COOPER.

JAMES FENIMORE COOPER was a person frequently filled to the bursting point with a diversity of indignations. He eased a steamy nature by suing, at one time or another, a large part of his acquaintanceship and, when not legally involved or writing novels, dashed off pamphlets that blasted human pretenses and transgressions.

Cooper spent much space and spleen in denunciation of the *Somers* affair and the conduct of his fellow author. As antidote to the several self-justifications Mackenzie composed, his voluntary and vehement adversary published two major attacks against the commander.

One of these verbal assaults and batteries was a booklet, not too succinctly entitled: "The Cruise of the *Somers*, Illustrative of the Despotism of the Quarterdeck and of the Unmanly Conduct of Commander Mackenzie." The other was a commentary included in a commercially issued transcript of Mackenzie's court-martial.

It may have been pure hatred of injustice that inspired the attacks; it may have been, in part, sympathy for the boy the captain of the *Somers* had hanged. The early lives of Cooper and Philip Spencer had been roughly parallel.

The author of the Leatherstocking novels had been a slovenly and defiant student himself who had been kicked out of Yale as an incorrigible. Following his involuntary departure from college, he had shipped before the mast on the merchant ship *Sterling*, out of Wiscasset, Maine, to learn seamanship. His education was strenuous and disheveling, for the vessel in her forty-day passage of the Atlantic was buffeted by one storm after another, but Cooper returned to America with a still-unappeased love for the sea.

In January, 1808, young James received his warrant as midshipman in the United States Navy and continued in the service until his marriage in 1811. He was qualified to estimate Mackenzie's defense, for, in this instance at least, he knew thoroughly what he was talking about.

Cooper did not believe there had been any actual intention to mutiny aboard the *Somers*. Furthermore, he intemperately considered the supplementary excuses for the three executions as advanced by the executioners just so much pusillanimous nonsense.

Mackenzie and his officers had presented four prime reasons why they had found it essential to hang three men. The earliest submitted of these had to do with the size and construction of the brig herself.

The commander, in his highly colored summation of his own defense, dwelt at length upon the incitations to mutiny presented by so small and fragile a vessel. There was no place aboard her, he contended, where prisoners might be safely kept. Her lower deck was divided into four compartments—berth deck, steerage, wardroom, and cabin—"*by only thin and frail partitions, through which a strong man could force his way from the brig's stem to her stern by the shove of a shoulder or the push of a foot.*"

It therefore was essential, Mackenzie maintained, to keep the prisoners on the after part of the *Somers'* top deck.

"*But the deck is flush, fore and aft and there the prisoners necessarily remained within a few feet of each other and in full sight of the crew. To prevent the prisoners from communicating with each other and the rest of the crew by words was difficult; to prevent such communication by signs was impossible.*"

This was contention one, and the officers of the brig unanimously endorsed it. Former Midshipman Cooper was not impressed. He considered these harmonious witnesses for the defense were poor sailors, or falsifiers, or both. Their denouncer wrote:

"*The size of the* Somers *was, perhaps, as near as possible to that which was the most desirable for her officers in the event of such conflict.... Place twenty men on a frigate's quarterdeck, and they could be turned, or assailed from so many points as to render them weak, but twenty, or even ten armed men on the quarterdeck of a brig of 266 tons make them a very formidable array as opposed to any number of unarmed men, or even armed men that could approach them at a time.*

"*The size of the* Somers *was favorable to her officers in another point of view. We see nothing to have prevented Captain Mackenzie from sending all but his officers below and of carrying the brig across the ocean, if needed, with the gentlemen of the quarterdeck alone.*"

As for "*the thin and frail partitions,*" Cooper prescribed that the first man tampering with them should have been shot from above.

"*The idea of men's knocking down bulkheads with fire-arms thrust through the gratings within six feet of their heads strikes us as being a little forced. . . . As for Captain Mackenzie's ability to send all hands below, who can doubt it when it is known that he made them hang three of their supposed ringleaders?"*

There were still other ways to have dealt with the alleged peril, and Mackenzie's critic obligingly supplied them. A rope might have been stretched thwartships at the break of the quarter-deck with the warning that any man who tried to cross it would be killed immediately. The guns of the *Somers'* batteries might all have been discharged, save the two aftermost carronades. These could have been loaded with canister, slued around, and pointed forward.

"We conceive that a vessel of the Somers' *size, under such circumstances, even admitting a pretty widespread disaffection to exist forward, would have the chances of nine in ten in favor of her officers, and that risk, it strikes us, might have been run before an American citizen was hanged without trial."*

Mackenzie's reports had described the dire increase in peril that each night's darkness had brought and witnesses for the defense had elaborated on that theme. Cooper was not having any.

"The answers to all these difficulties are very simple. In the first place, there was no necessity for darkness, every man-of-war possessing means of lighting her decks. In the next place, there was no necessity for a single individual of the crew coming on the quarterdeck at all."

In contention two, Mackenzie held that the rapidly increasing disaffection of the crew had made imperative the immediate hanging of Spencer, Cromwell, and Small.

"The sullenness and moroseness, the violent and menacing

demeanor and the portentous looks of the crew between the arrest of Mr. Spencer and the execution are not the creations of fancy. Every officer and many of the seamen have sworn to their existence. . . . They observed the ominous appearances from hour to hour and from day to day and watched with care their fearful progress."

And why, Cooper wanted to know, should not the crew have appeared disorganized and apprehensive after the ostentation that had accompanied Spencer's arrest?

"We entertain no doubt that much the greater portion of the ominous conversations, groupings, shakings of the head and strange looks, which seem to have awakened so much distrust aft, had their origin in the natural wonder of the crew at seeing an officer in this novel situation; and he, too, not only a favorite forward but one who was known to be the son of a minister of state. . . . The men collected in knots together, it is said, and conversed together, separating as the officers approached and would look aft at the prisoner seated on the arms chest.

"These facts have been dwelt on by some commentators in a way, we think, to show that they were striving after evidence of danger, rather than after sober truth. The Somers had one hundred and twenty souls aboard her—at least thirty more than she should have had—and it is scarcely possible that, with her boats stowed and one third of her deck reserved for her officers, one hundred men could be on her remaining deck without being in what is called 'knots.' We should have considered a contrary course as affording much the strongest proofs of a conspiracy."

Mackenzie, in contention three, opposed the idea that the prisoners should or could have been put ashore at St. Thomas and the brig freed of their contamination. He denounced this expedient on ethical and geographical grounds, and his officers, as usual, sustained him.

"*An American ship-of-war*," the commander informed his court-martial, "*is always deemed competent to meet an enemy from without of a force not superior to her own; much more should she be deemed competent to meet and quell, by her own power, an enemy from within.*

"*If she is not capable of maintaining her own discipline, she ought not to be held worthy to fight her country's battles. It would seem a degradation to our flag* [the practically omnipresent flag!] *for an American ship-of-war to invoke the aid of a foreign government to sustain the discipline or quell the insurrection of her crew.*"

Moreover, any discussion as to whether it would have been better to uphold the proprieties or to spare human lives was, according to the commander, beside the point.

"*The evidence repels the supposition that the* Somers *could have reached St. Thomas with all the prisoners alive. There was every reason to believe that what the conspirators intended to do they would do quickly. Mr. Wales had understood from Mr. Spencer that the mutiny was to take place very shortly and even before their arrival at St. Thomas.*"

Mr. Wales, it is worth remembering, forgot to mention that important circumstance to anyone until months after the execution.

There were islands nearer to the brig than St. Thomas on December 1. According to Sailing Master Perry's calculations, at noon of that day, Barbados, Antigua, Guadeloupe, Dominica, and St. Lucia were less than two days' average sailing time away. Nevertheless, Mackenzie insisted that it not only would have been flag-soiling but also suicidal to have altered the *Somers'* course and to have run for the nearest harbor.

"*The sudden departure from the known course of the voyage would have been virtually an official admission that the mutiny was too strong for the authorities of the ship and that the bearing away was but a flight from the dreaded danger to crave protection from the government on shore.*

"*Such an admission, while it would have disheartened the faithful, could not have failed to give strength to the ranks of the faithless.*"

The commander's officer witnesses sustained without hesitation contention three, but again Mr. Cooper flatly disagreed. It was his emphatic belief "*that, the instant the commander of the* Somers *foresaw a probable necessity of executing the prisoners, it became his duty to stand for the nearest available port....*"

"*It is not true that a man-of-war will not seek protection in a friendly port in grave emergencies. It is done constantly in peace or in war. Protection is sought in this way from the elements, from the horrors of starvation, and why not mutineers? ... The question is narrowed down to this: Ought Captain Mackenzie and his officers in order to avoid the grievous necessity of hanging American citizens without trial—nay, without a hearing—to submit to a mortification of their professional pride?*"

If, as Mackenzie insisted, the knowledge that the *Somers* had altered her course and was running toward a refuge would have destroyed the confidence of his subordinates, why then, Cooper snorted, they must have been most peculiar officers. He pursued:

"*As it was, they were armed to the teeth, were pointing pistols at the men and threatening to shoot them and were existing in anything but a quiet, calm confidence of the power of discipline. . . . It must have been a strange set of officers who did not understand the difference between going into port in order to avoid the necessity of hanging men without trial and of going into port out of apprehension of the crew."*

Mackenzie had submitted, as contention four, that his subordinates had been coming apart rapidly under the ordeal of standing watch-and-watch about—four-hour spells of duty with only four-hour rest periods between them.

"They stood sentinels on the deck and ultimately had no alternative but to remain there under arms day and night, watch-and-watch about. To the refreshing influence of quiet sleep they had become strangers. Fatigue and consuming care were wasting away their youthful frames. Nature could have endured the struggle but little longer."

To this argument the lately wasted officers of the *Somers* had returned by their united testimony a fervent "Amen."

"Bilge!" said Mr. Cooper, in effect, and added autobiographical detail to his rebuttal.

"What was there to cause all this exhaustion? These gentlemen were on watch-and-watch. So are thousands of others daily. We have ourselves, at a tender age, too, been watch-and-watch for weeks and weeks and had our rest broken, night after night in addition, to help make and shorten sail. It is a common thing to be all hands all day and watch-and-watch at night for long voyages.

"But these gentlemen had to carry pistols and a cutlass. Is this harder on the human frame than to add the labor of ship's duty to the watch-and-watch of ordinary sailors?

"But these gentlemen could not sleep on account of the uneasiness natural to their situation. . . . We have a better opinion of the physical powers of these gentlemen than they

*have themselves.... As for the fatigue produced by walking
so much, to which some of them allude, Captain Mackenzie
should have permitted them to sit down."*

Having dealt with the principal contentions advanced by
the executioner-in-chief to justify his deed, Mackenzie's most
eminent public critic luffed to rake him. Without mercy and
for a number of pages, Cooper blew apart lesser pretenses and
mendacities presented by the commander and endorsed by
his echoing officers. Before the assailant bore away, he fired
a concluding broadside into the wreckage:

*"Many imagine that Captain Mackenzie's report betrays
the evidence of a disposition to gain personal renown, from
the manner in which it is pretended he saved his own life and
those of his associates. The feebleness of this extraordinary
document renders its writer obnoxious [sic] to very injurious
suspicions, certainly, and this among the number, but the
mental obliquity, so very obvious throughout the whole affair,
renders any ordinary analysis of human motives exceedingly
precarious.*

*"God alone can say how far any selfish feeling was mixed
up with the mistakes of this terrible transaction."*

James Fenimore Cooper's philippic was published in 1844.
One hundred and ten subsequent years have yielded no warrant for a more positive judgment.

On December 15, 1843, exactly a year and a day from the
time when the *Somers* had returned to New York with her
terrific tidings, Commander Alexander Slidell Mackenzie
picked up his seldom-idle pen and wrote a letter to his nephew
and former clerk. The talkative young Oliver H. Perry had
failed to obtain any appointment in the navy and had found

occupation in New Orleans, close to the families of his uncle, John Slidell, and of his old shipmate, Adrien Deslonde.

"*My dear Oliver*," the commander wrote in his small, prim hand, "*I have been for some time desirous of sending Mr. Deslonde a pair of Berkshire pigs which I reserved for him soon after your letter on the subject of pigs was received last summer. It would have freighted a small vessel to have sent all you wrote for, had they been forthcoming. They are shipped aboard the* Huntsville *to sail on the 20th instant. I have notified Mr. Deslonde of their being sent, but if he should not be in town, will you attend to forwarding them?*

"*The pigs will be placed in the charge of a little boy and he will be told that if he takes care of them, he will have a gratuity of a dollar. If they are not in good condition when they arrive, give him nothing, for they are shipped in the highest possible order.*

"*I hope you are studying and working industriously. Your future success and responsibility in life, affecting yourself first and then your family and friends, depend wholly on yourself. Bear this in mind. Be modest. Believe that you have everything to learn and then you will be sure to learn something.*"

Whether he was shipping pigs or hanging members of his crew, Commander Mackenzie was always able to wring a moral preachment from the enterprise.

Bibliography

Records of Officers, 1840–48. Department of the Navy, National Archives, Washington, D.C.

Letters to Officers—Ships of War, December 9, 1842–May 16, 1843. Department of the Navy, National Archives, Washington, D.C.

John C. Spencer Letters, Miscellaneous Papers, 1811–49. New York Public Library, New York.

Naval Papers, 1837–44. New York Public Library, New York.

George Walgrove Warner Papers, in author's possession.

New York Tribune, December 1, 1842–May 1, 1843. New York.

New York Herald, December 1, 1842–May 1, 1843. New York.

New York Courier & Enquirer, December 1, 1842–May 1, 1843. New York.

"Inquiry into the *Somers* Mutiny." New York: 1843.

"Case of the *Somers* Mutiny; Defense of Alexander Slidell Mackenzie." New York: 1843.

"Proceedings of the Naval Court Martial in the Case of Alexander Slidell Mackenzie, with a Review by James Fenimore Cooper." New York: 1844.

ADAMS, GRACE, and HUTTER, EDWARD. *The Mad Forties*. New York: Harper & Brothers, 1942.

BENJAMIN, PARK. *The United States Naval Academy*. New York: G. P. Putnam's Sons, 1900.

BENTON, THOMAS HART. *Thirty Years' View*. New York: 1856.

BILL, ALFRED HOYT. *Rehearsal for Conflict*. New York: Alfred A. Knopf, Inc., 1947.

CHAPELLE, HOWARD I. *History of the American Sailing Navy*. New York: W. W. Norton & Company, Inc., 1949.

COOPER, JAMES FENIMORE. *The Cruise of the* Somers. New York: 1844.

GAY, WILLIAM W. "Some Recollections of Spencer," *The Purple and Gold*, Magazine of the Chi Psi Fraternity, Vol. II, No. 3. April, 1885.

GRIFFIN, ERNEST FREELAND, editor. *Westchester County and Its People*. New York: 1846.

HARWOOD, REAR ADMIRAL ANDREW A. *Law and Practice of United States Naval Court Martial*. New York: 1867.

IRVING, PIERRE M. *The Life and Letters of Washington Irving*. New York: 1864.

MACKENZIE, ALEXANDER SLIDELL. *A Year in Spain*. London: 1831.

———. *The American in England*. New York: 1835.

———. *Popular Essays on Naval Subjects*. New York: 1833.

———. *Spain Revisited*. New York: 1836.

———. *Life of Commodore Oliver H. Perry*. New York: 1840.

———. *Life of John Paul Jones*. New York: 1845.

———. *Life of Commodore Stephen Decatur*. Boston: 1846.

PRATT, FLETCHER. *The Navy*. New York: Garden City Pub. Co., Inc., 1941.

———. *Preble's Boys*. New York: William Sloane Associates, Inc., 1950.

SEWARD, WILLIAM H. *Autobiography*. New York: 1871.

WEED, THURLOW. *Autobiography*. Boston: 1883.

WOODWARD, WILLIAM E. *The Way Our People Lived*. New York: E. P. Dutton & Co., Inc., 1944.